TOP RAMEN NOODLE COOKBOOK

*Over 175 Delicious, Quick,
Easy, and Inexpensive
Recipes Using
America's Favorite Noodle*

Elizabeth Prungel
and
Heather Spyker

P Prima Publishing
P.O. Box 1260
Rocklin, CA 95677

To our mothers, Mrs. Anita LaCoff and Mrs. Kathy Dellinger. Thank you for your inspiration, instruction, support, and love.

Top Ramen® and Top Ramen® Low Fat are registered products of Nissin Foods (USA) Co., Inc., Fort Lee, New Jersey.

Copyediting by Janis Paris
Production by Andi Reese Brady
Design and composition by Archetype Book Composition
Cover design by Lindy Dunlavey, The Dunlavey Studio, Inc.

Library of Congress Cataloging-in-Publication Data

Prungel, Elizabeth.
    Top Ramen Noodle Cookbook: over 175 delicious, quick, easy, and inexpensive recipes using America's favorite noodle / Elizabeth Prungel, Heather Spyker.
        p.   cm.
    Includes index.
    ISBN 1-55958-565-X
    1. Cookery (pasta)   2. Noodles.   I. Spyker, Heather.   II. Title.
TX809.M17P78   1994
641.8′22—dc20

94-21450
CIP

95 96 97 RRD 10 9 8 7 6 5 4 3 2 1
Printed in the United States of America

How to Order:
Single copies may be ordered from Prima Publishing, P.O. Box 1260BK, Rocklin, CA 95677; telephone (916) 632-4400. Quantity discounts are also available. On your letterhead, include information concerning the intended use of the books and the number of books you wish to purchase.

CONTENTS

ACKNOWLEDGMENTS

We would like to thank the following people for giving us ideas or recipes to use in our book: Kathy Dellinger, Ruth Dellinger, Wayne Spyker, Kathy and Chris Eisenhart, Virginia Burns, Jason Burns, Frances Ferguson Knoepp, Rich Elder, Rich Broderick, Anita and Bill LaCoff, Hank Dombrowski, and Oma Prunger. Heartiest thanks to our families for their love, patience, and understanding.

We also thank our agent, Bill Adler, for his ideas and support. Appreciation goes to our publisher, Prima Publishing, especially our publicist, Jenn Nelson.

Finally, we thank anyone who, in some way, encouraged the writing of this book.

PREFACE

As roommates in our sophomore year of college, we were known for our culinary masterpieces in the dormitory kitchen (one burner, one sink). We learned that college students *can* make real meals almost as good as their mothers made at home with a lot less time and effort.

Ramen noodles were a key ingredient in many of our quick-and-easy recipes. They are a staple that can be purchased at any grocery store, usually for the bargain price of six for $1.00—a buy even starving college students can afford. Ramen noodles have resisted inflation better than any other product in America. While there's no such thing as a free lunch, with ramen noodes, there is an almost-free lunch!

There are dozens of varieties of ramen noodles, ranging from plain to sizzlingly spicy, from lowfat, air-dried ones to prefried. *Top Ramen Noodle Cookbook* describes these varieties and helps you select which to use.

The recipes that follow represent new and innovative ways to prepare Top Ramen and Top Ramen Low Fat noodles. We have endeavored to reinvent the image of ramen noodles. Most of the following recipes are easy; they usually require only one or two pans, and the additional ingredients are inexpensive and readily available. Although we suggest Top Ramen, any brand of ramen noodle can be used.

We hope these recipes give your ramen (and your imagination) new life and give you a new perspective on economical cuisine. Boil a pot of water and enjoy!

INTRODUCTION

A BRIEF HISTORY OF RAMEN NOODLES

The origins of ramen noodles are Chinese, although they have also become a part of Japanese cuisine. The Chinese may have enjoyed the first ramen noodles made of wheat as early as 100 B.C., and the first written ramen recipe dates from the sixth century.

Instant ramen noodles were created in 1958 by Momofuko Ando, the founder and chairman of Nissin Foods Co., Inc. Before this time, noodles were sent to markets fresh and lasted only two days.

People have been eating ramen noodles for centuries, and their popularity is on the rise. According to *Supermarket News* (23 March 1992), ramen noodle sales have been increasing at a rate of 12 percent for the past ten years. The following recipes should guarantee that you, too, will enjoy ramen noodles for a long time to come.

HOW TO CHOOSE YOUR RAMEN

One of ramen's great advantages is that they are an easy and inexpensive way to fill you up. Ramen also adapt well to almost any recipe. Another little-discussed advantage of ramen is that they are a wonderful way to get carbohydrates into your diet. Some readers may be concerned with what else goes into ramen. Ramen do contain sodium, though most people find they especially like a touch of salt on starchy foods like pasta and potatoes. Ramen also contain some MSG, a food additive harmless to all but a few individuals who have an allergy to MSG.

For those who must carefully watch their diets, look for Top Ramen Low Fat from Nissin Food Co., the makers of Top Ramen. Top Ramen Low Fat is a great tasting line of ramen that uses air and microwave drying. This new product has lower fat than regular ramen, is low in saturated fat, and has no cholesterol. It is currently available in many areas of the country.

DRESSING UP YOUR RAMEN

In this, the age of eat and run, ramen noodles seem a god-send. They are quick, easy, and inexpensive to make. To add an extra touch to your ramen, try topping your recipes with ground pepper or cheese. Garnishing should be a fun part of the meal, too. It never hurts to put a beautiful lettuce leaf under a cold ramen salad or slice some cucumbers to sit on a place with a helping of ramen casserole. If you live alone or with a roommate, one or two nice plates also help spruce up a meal.

Ramen is an excellent dish for your own experimentation. For a sauce, try using some of those condiments and foods that you usually have on hand, like butter, spaghetti sauce, Cheese Whiz®, and even—for the kids—ketchup! Remember, when mixing something into ramen, it's best to break the noodles into quarters—they mix better that way.

HELPFUL HINTS

The following is a list of terms frequently used in this book:

Prepare noodles as directed
Boil 1 package of noodles in 2 cups of water for 3 minutes.

Broken into 4 pieces
We think this is pretty self-explanatory.

Coarsely broken
Break up noodle block but don't take out all the curls.

Crushed
Take out all the curls in the noodles.

Finely crushed
Pulvarize the noodles.

Packets of soy sauce, Chinese hot mustard, and duck sauce
In some of our recipes, we use packets of these sauces that we have left over from takeout Chinese food. If you don't have an abundance of these leftover packets, each one is equal to approximately 1 tablespoon.

We are unashamed big eaters. Thus our serving suggestions may be a little over the FDA's recommendations, but we think they're realistic.

Concerning seasoning packets, you can add the seasoning packet to the water in which the noodles are boiled, or you can boil the noodles in plain water, drain, and then add the seasoning packet. Whichever way you choose is fine with us. Unless a method is specified, our recipes work for both methods.

APPETIZERS

Let Top Ramen noodles begin your party; surprise your guests with appetizers made with ramen noodles. The following appetizers range from casual to sophisticated, and they're quick and easy—just like the noodles themselves.

"TOP YOUR OWN" RAMEN

1. Prepare several packages of Top Ramen or Top Ramen Low Fat (amount depends on the number of guests).
2. Put out bowls of toppings so guests can choose how to top their own noodles.

Suggestions for toppings:

Chopped scallions

Diced tomatoes

Soy sauce

Spaghetti sauce

Grated or shredded cheese

Spices (garlic powder, oregano, basil)

Bacon bits

Chopped olives

RAMEN-TOPPED BISCUITS

1   package (7 ounces) refrigerated biscuits
(containing 10 biscuits)
1   tablespoon butter, melted
1/3   package Top Ramen or Top Ramen
Low Fat, crushed, (no seasoning packet)

1. Heat oven to 450°F.
2. Grease 9-inch round cake pan. Separate dough into 10 biscuits. Arrange biscuits in pan. Brush with melted butter.
3. Sprinkle biscuits with raw ramen and gently press noodles down into biscuits.
4. Bake at 450°F for 8–10 minutes or until biscuits begin to brown at edges. Serve warm with butter or honey.

Yield: 10 servings

SESAME RAMEN

1   package Top Ramen or Top Ramen
     Low Fat (no seasoning packet)
1   tablespoon sesame oil
1/3 cup chopped carrots
1   tablespoon sesame seeds

1. Prepare noodles as directed. Drain.
2. Toss noodles with sesame oil, carrots, and sesame seeds.
3. Chill about 2 hours or until cold.

Yield: 1 serving

RAMEN
SNACK MIX

4	tablespoons (1/2 stick) butter
1 1/4	teaspoons seasoned salt
4 1/2	teaspoons Worcestershire sauce
4	cups crispy rice or corn squares cereal
2	packages Top Ramen or Top Ramen Low Fat, crushed (no seasoning packet)
1	cup peanuts
1	cup small or bite-size pretzels

1. Melt butter.
2. In a small bowl, combine salt, Worcestershire sauce, and melted butter; mix well.
3. Pour sauce, cereal, uncooked ramen, peanuts, and pretzels into large plastic bag and close securely. Shake bag until all pieces are coated.
4. Pour contents of bag into large microwave-safe bowl. Microwave on high for 6 minutes, stirring every 2 minutes.

5. Spread mix evenly on paper towels to cool.
6. Store in an airtight container.

≈**NOTE**≈ If you'd rather use an oven, after mixing ingredients in bag pour them evenly into an open roasting pan. Bake at 250°F for 1 hour, stirring every 15 minutes. Follow same cooling directions.

Yield: 5 servings

ROSEMARY RAMEN TART

1   package Top Ramen or Top Ramen
       Low Fat (no seasoning packet)
1/2   teaspoon dried rosemary
2   tablespoons butter
1/2   cup shredded mozzarella cheese
1/2   cup green olives, chopped

1. Prepare noodles as directed. Drain.
2. Toss noodles with rosemary and 1 tablespoon of the butter.
3. Melt second tablespoon of butter in small fry pan and press noodles into pan (see "Fried Ramen" recipe, page 31). Bring heat to medium low and fry for about 15 minutes until the noodles are crisp on the bottom.
4. Before serving, top with the cheese and olives.
5. Cut into small wedges.

Yield: 1 or 2 servings

RAMEN
CHEESE SQUARES

3	packages Top Ramen or Top Ramen Low Fat (no seasoning packet)
1	can condensed cheddar cheese soup
1/2	soup can of milk
1	teaspoon chili powder
	Salt and pepper to taste

1. Preheat oven to 375°F.

2. Prepare noodles as directed. Drain.

3. Mix noodles with cheddar cheese soup, milk, and chili powder until noodles are coated.

4. Pour mixture evenly into a greased 9-inch square cake pan. Bake for 25 minutes or until semisolid.

5. Let cool for at least an hour. Cut into squares.

Yield: 10–15 squares

HERB NOODLE BITES

2   different seasoning packets
1/4 cup bread crumbs
1   egg, beaten
2   tablespoons milk
1   package Top Ramen or Top Ramen
     Low Fat, coarsely broken (any flavor)

1. Mix seasoning packets and bread crumbs together in shallow bowl.

2. Stir together egg and milk.

3. Drop tablespoons of uncooked noodles into egg mixture and coat.

4. Then drop into crumb mixture and coat.

5. Place noodle bites onto nonstick cookie sheet or cake pan. Bake at 375°F about 12–15 minutes or until crispy. Keep checking so they don't burn.

6. Serve in bowl as finger food.

Yield: 3 servings

RAMEN
CHEESE BALL

2	cloves garlic, minced
1/2	cup butter, softened (1 stick)
8	ounces cream cheese, softened
4	teaspoons white wine vinegar
4	teaspoons basil
1 1/2	tablespoons freshly ground black pepper
1	package Top Ramen or Top Ramen Low Fat, crushed (no seasoning packet)

1. Whip together all ingredients except pepper and ramen in blender or with hand mixer.
2. Roll mixture into ball and coat with pepper and ramen.
3. Refrigerate at least 1 hour. Serve with crackers and/or raw vegetables.

Yield: 4 servings

PASTA PESTO
MOLD

2   packages Top Ramen or Top Ramen
         Low Fat, crushed (no seasoning packet)
1 1/2 cups pesto sauce (see page 35)
1   teaspoon fresh basil (optional garnish)

1. Prepare noodles as directed. Drain.
2. Line a 4-cup mold with plastic wrap. Spread half the pesto in mold. Top with half the noodles. Next spread the other half of the pesto; finish with last layer of noodles.
3. Chill 6–24 hours.
4. To serve, unmold on plate. Remove plastic wrap.
5. Garnish with fresh basil. Serve with knife and crackers.

Yield: 6 servings

RAMEN
LATKES

1	package Top Ramen or Top Ramen Low Fat, crushed (any flavor)
2	medium potatoes
1	small onion
2	eggs, beaten
1	teaspoon each salt and pepper Cooking oil, enough for 2 inches in a medium (2-quart) saucepan

1. Prepare noodles as directed with seasoning packet. Set aside.

2. Peel and grate potatoes. Grate onion.

3. Mix potatoes and onion, and put them in colander, squeezing out all moisture.

4. Then mix potato mixture with noodles, eggs, salt, and pepper.

5. Heat oven to 300°F.

6. Heat oil in saucepan. With a spoon, drop spoonfuls of mixture into hot oil. After about 20 seconds, press down balls into thin pancakes. As they brown, turn them over to cook other side.

7. As they are cooked, remove pancakes and put them on paper towels to drain. Keep warm in oven.

8. Serve with applesauce or sour cream.

PARTY MEATBALLS

1	egg, beaten
1	can condensed tomato soup, divided
1	package Top Ramen or Top Ramen Low Fat, crushed (beef flavor)
1/4	teaspoon garlic powder
1/4	teaspoon onion powder
1/4	teaspoon pepper
1	lb. ground beef
1	teaspoon Worcestershire sauce
1/2	teaspoon oregano
1/2	cup water
	Grated Parmesan cheese

1. Combine egg, 1/2 can of the soup, raw ramen, garlic powder, onion powder, pepper, and beef. Mix well.

2. Shape beef mixture into 20 meatballs. Place them in large skillet.

3. Mix remaining soup with Worcestershire sauce, oregano, and water. Pour over meatballs. Bring mixture to a boil.

4. Reduce heat. Cover and simmer, stirring often, for about 20 minutes until no pink remains in meat and noodles are tender.

5. Skim fat.

6. Top with Parmesan cheese before serving.

FRIED NOODLE
PIZZA

1	package Top Ramen or Top Ramen Low Fat (any flavor)
1	tablespoon butter
2	tablespoons spaghetti sauce
1	ounce (several slices, depending on size) pepperoni
2	tablespoons canned, drained mushrooms
2	tablespoons shredded mozzarella cheese

1. Prepare noodles as directed. Drain.
2. Prepare "Fried Ramen" by pressing drained noodles into saucepan containing melted butter. (See "Fried Ramen" recipe, page 31.)
3. When bottom begins to crisp, spread on top of the noodles the spaghetti sauce, a couple of slices pepperoni, mushrooms, and cheese.
4. Let cheese melt and all toppings warm up. Be careful not to burn bottom of noodles.

Yield: 1 serving

Soups

You can stir cooked Top Ramen or Top Ramen Low Fat noodles into regular canned soups to make the soups more hearty. We have used chicken noodle soup and beef vegetable. Try adding cooked ramen to soups you like.

In addition, try the following recipes for soups with ramen as one of the main ingredients.

EGG DROP SOUP WITH NOODLES

4	cups water
1	package Top Ramen or Top Ramen Low Fat (chicken flavor)
1	egg, beaten

1. In a 2-quart saucepan, boil water and seasoning packet.
2. Add noodles and boil for 3 minutes.
3. Reduce heat to simmering. Gently stir in the egg. Stir slowly as egg forms light fluffy pieces.

≈**NOTE**≈ You can also leave ramen out of this recipe and use only the seasoning packet to make a broth in which to drop beaten egg.

Yield: 2 servings

BRUSSELS SPROUT SOUP

1/4   pound smoked kielbasa
1/2   pound brussels sprouts
4   cups water
1   package Top Ramen or Top Ramen
        Low Fat (pork flavor)
        Salt and pepper to taste

1. Slice the kielbasa into bite-size pieces.
2. Peel the leaves from the brussels sprouts; discard the centers.
3. Boil water with seasoning packet.
4. Add kielbasa and brussels sprout leaves to boiling water. Boil 3–5 minutes.
5. Add ramen. Cover and simmer 10 minutes or until brussels sprouts are tender. Season to taste.

Yield: 2 servings

RAMEN CABBAGE SOUP

1 1/2 tablespoons butter
1/2 medium head cabbage, shredded (about 2 cups)
2 carrots, julienned
1 small onion, minced
1 clove garlic, minced
5 cups water
1/4 teaspoon pepper
1 package Top Ramen or Top Ramen Low Fat, crushed (chicken flavor)

1. In a Dutch oven or large pan, sauté butter, cabbage, carrots, onion, and garlic for 8 minutes.

2. Add water, pepper, seasoning packet, and crushed ramen.

3. Cover and simmer for 30 minutes or until vegetables are tender.

Yield: 4 servings

PEPPERONI PIZZA SOUP

2	tablespoons olive oil
1	small onion, chopped
1/2	cup fresh mushrooms, sliced
1/2	cup green pepper, chopped
1/2	cup pepperoni slices
2	cloves garlic
2	cups beef broth (or 2 beef seasoning packets and water)
1	cup tomato sauce
1	teaspoon basil
2	packages Top Ramen or Top Ramen Low Fat (no seasoning packet)
1/4	cup shredded mozzarella cheese

1. In a medium saucepan, sauté onions, mushrooms, green pepper, pepperoni, and garlic in olive oil until tender.
2. Add broth, tomato sauce, basil, and raw noodles. Simmer for about 10 minutes or until mixture thickens.
3. Top with mozzarella.

Yield: 4 servings

EASY HOMEMADE CHICKEN VEGETABLE SOUP

2	tablespoons olive oil
1	cup chopped carrots
1	cup chopped celery
1	cup chopped onion
1	cup cut green beans
2	cups water
2	(16 ounce) cans commercial chicken broth
1	whole chicken breast, deboned, cut into bite-size pieces
2	packages Top Ramen or Top Ramen Low Fat (chicken flavor)

1. In a large saucepan, sauté carrots, celery, onion, and green beans in oil until just cooked (onion should be translucent).
2. Add water, chicken broth, seasoning packets, and chicken and bring to a boil.
3. Reduce heat and simmer 20 minutes stirring occasionally.
4. Meanwhile, prepare noodles as directed. Drain.
5. Stir noodles into soup and heat through.

Yield: 4 servings

EASY HOMEMADE VEGETABLE SOUP

2	tablespoons olive oil
1	cup broccoli florets
1	cup coarsely chopped carrots
1	cup cut green beans
2/3	cup chopped celery
1/2	cup chopped onion
1/4	cup diced green pepper
2	tablespoons dried parsley
3	cloves garlic, minced
2	(16 ounce) cans commercial chicken broth
2	bay leaves
1	teaspoon dried chopped chives
2	packages Top Ramen or Top Ramen Low Fat (no seasoning packet)

1. In a large saucepan, sauté vegetables, parsley, and garlic in oil until vegetables just begin to cook.
2. Add broth, bay leaves, and chives; bring to a boil.
3. Reduce heat and simmer 20 minutes.
4. Return soup to a boil and add raw noodles, stirring occasionally until noodles are tender.
5. Remove bay leaves before serving.

Yield: 4 servings

RAMEN PASTA SOUP

1/2	pound ground beef
2	cups tomato juice
2	cups water
1	teaspoon salt
1/4	teaspoon garlic salt
1/4	teaspoon pepper
1	tablespoon instant beef bouillon (1 cube)
1/2	green pepper, minced
1/2	small onion, minced
1	small can (7 oz.) stewed tomatoes
1	cup shredded cabbage
2	packages Top Ramen or Top Ramen Low Fat (no seasoning packet)
1	cup frozen mixed vegetables (about 8 ounces)

1. In a large saucepan, brown ground beef and drain grease.

2. Stir in juice, water, seasonings, boullion, green pepper, onion, tomatoes, and cabbage. Bring to a boil.

3. Reduce heat and simmer for 30 minutes or until vegetables are tender.

4. Prepare noodles as directed. Drain.

5. Stir frozen vegetables and noodles into soup mixture. Heat thoroughly.

Yield: 4 servings

RAMEN AND BEAN SOUP

1/4	pound ground beef
2	medium carrots, thinly sliced
2	medium celery stalks, thinly sliced
1	medium red pepper, diced
1	small onion, chopped
1/4	teaspoon dried basil
	Pinch of salt
1	can (16 ounces) cannelini beans
1	can (14 ounces) beef broth
1	cup water
1	package Top Ramen or Top Ramen Low Fat (beef flavor)
1	cup fresh chopped spinach
1/4	pound (1/3 cup) grated Parmesan cheese

1. In a Dutch oven or large saucepan, brown ground beef; drain grease.

2. Add carrots, celery, red pepper, onion, basil, and salt; cook, stirring occasionally, until vegetables are still slightly crisp.

3. Meanwhile, rinse and drain cannelini beans. In a medium bowl, mash beans until smooth. Stir mashed beans into vegetable mixture. Add beef broth and water and heat to boiling.

4. Add raw ramen and seasoning packet and cook uncovered for 6–8 minutes, stirring occasionally until ramen and vegetables are thoroughly tender.
5. Stir in spinach; heat through.
6. Sprinkle with grated Parmesan cheese.

Yield: 4 servings

ENTREES WITHOUT MEAT

We call these recipes "entrees without meat" and not "vegetarian" because if seasoning packets are used in a recipe, that recipe is not vegetarian. All seasoning packets contain some animal product; an example is chicken powder in the vegetable flavor Top Ramen. If you don't use seasoning packets, then your dish can be considered truly vegetarian.

Many of these dishes can be thought of as building blocks—you can experiment by adding meat to any nonmeat recipe.

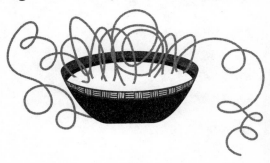

FRIED
RAMEN

1   package Top Ramen or Top Ramen
       Low Fat (any flavor)
1   tablespoon oil

1. Prepare noodles as directed. Drain (reserving 2 table-spoons of the liquid).
2. Mix noodles with reserved liquid.
3. Heat oil in a small fry pan (you don't need oil if you have a nonstick pan). When the pan is hot, add the noodles, pressing them firmly down into the pan.
4. Reduce heat to low and let the noodles fry until the bottom is crispy and the top is warmed through (about 15 minutes).
5. Cut into pie-shaped wedges and serve. Apple slices or processed cheese spread are a nice accompaniment.

Yield: 1 serving

FRIED RAMEN WITH SPINACH OR KALE

1	package Top Ramen or Top Ramen Low Fat (any flavor)
3/4	cup chopped frozen spinach or kale
1	tablespoon vinegar

1. Prepare "Fried Ramen" recipe (see page 31).
2. Thaw spinach or kale in a colander and squeeze out all excess water.
3. Press the fried noodles into the fry pan, spreading the spinach or kale within half an inch of the sides of the noodles.
4. When the bottom is crispy and the top is warmed through, sprinkle the top with vinegar.

≈**NOTE**≈ In place of vinegar, you might prefer to sprinkle the spinach with Parmesan cheese, some bread crumbs, and pepper.

Yield: 1 serving

FRIED RAMEN WITH VEGETABLES IN LIGHT SAUCE

2	packages Top Ramen or Top Ramen Low Fat (1 oriental flavor packet)
2	tablespoons oil, divided
2	tablespoons water
1	packet soy sauce
1/4	cup sliced mushrooms
1/4	cup sliced scallions
1	cup shredded cabbage

1. Prepare noodles as directed, reserving seasoning packet.

2. Make "Fried Ramen" recipe (see page 31), using one tablespoon of the oil.

3. When noodles are crispy on one side, flip the patty to brown on the second side.

4. Meanwhile in another fry pan, heat remaining tablespoon of oil, water, soy sauce, and seasoning packet. Add vegetables to sauce mixture and sauté for 7 minutes.

5. Serve on top of twice-browned noodles.

Yield: 3 servings

RAMEN TOSSED WITH GARLIC AND SPICES

1	package Top Ramen or Top Ramen Low Fat (no seasoning packet)
1	tablespoon olive oil
1	clove garlic, minced
1/4	cup grated Parmesan cheese
1	tablespoon crushed oregano

1. Prepare noodles as directed. Drain.
2. Sauté garlic, Parmesan cheese, and oregano in oil for 2 minutes.
3. Toss noodles with garlic mixture.

Yield: 1 serving

RAMEN TOSSED WITH PESTO

1	package Top Ramen or Top Ramen Low Fat (no seasoning packet)
1/3	cup commercial pesto
1/4	teaspoon coarsely ground pepper
1/2	teaspoon grated Parmesan cheese

1. Prepare noodles as directed. Drain.
2. Toss noodles with pesto; add pepper.
3. Sprinkle Parmesan cheese on top before serving.

Yield: 1 serving

≈**NOTE**≈ To make your own pesto, here's an easy recipe:

1	cup packed fresh basil leaves
1	large clove garlic
2	tablespoons pine nuts
	Dash salt
1/4	cup olive oil
1/4	cup Parmesan cheese
1	tablespoon butter, softened

1. Mix all ingredients but cheese and butter in a blender until smooth.
2. Add cheese and butter and process 10 more seconds.

EASY RAMEN
MEXICALI

1	package Top Ramen or Top Ramen Low Fat (chicken flavor)
2	tablespoons salsa
3	tablespoons processed cheese spread

1. Prepare noodles as directed. Drain.
2. Add salsa and cheese to ramen and mix well.

Yield: 1 serving

EASY RAMEN PUTTANESCA

1	package Top Ramen or Top Ramen Low Fat (any flavor)
1	tablespoon butter
1/4	teaspoon garlic powder
1/4	cup sliced black olives
1/2	cup tomato sauce
	Dash each: parsley, black pepper, ground red pepper

1. Prepare noodles as directed. Drain.
2. Melt butter in a saucepan. Add garlic powder and olives; sauté 2 minutes.
3. Add tomato sauce and spices and cook 3 more minutes.
4. Mix noodles with sauce and serve.

Yield: 1 serving

RAMEN WITH SAUTÉED TOMATO AND GARLIC

1	tablespoon oil or butter
2	cloves of garlic, minced
1	medium tomato, diced
1	teaspoon crushed dried oregano
1	package Top Ramen or Top Ramen Low Fat (chicken flavor)

1. In a small fry pan, sauté the garlic in the oil, stirring frequently—be careful not to burn.
2. When the garlic is golden, add the tomato and oregano. Turn heat to low, cover and simmer.
3. While tomato mixture is simmering, prepare noodles as directed, reserving seasoning packet. Drain.
4. Return noodles to saucepan. Add tomato mixture and seasoning packet. Toss and serve.

Yield: 1 serving

PEPPER CABBAGE SAUTÉ

1	package Top Ramen or Top Ramen Low Fat, broken into 4 pieces (pork flavor)
2	tablespoons butter
1/4	small head of cabbage, shredded (about 3/4 cup)
	Dash each: salt, pepper, and garlic powder

1. Prepare noodles as directed. Drain.
2. Sauté the cabbage and spices in butter for 15 minutes over medium heat, stirring occasionally.
3. Combine with ramen and serve.

Yield: 1 serving

ORIENTAL RAMEN

1	cup frozen mixed vegetables (about 8 ounces)
1	package Top Ramen or Top Ramen Low Fat, coarsely broken (oriental flavor)
1	packet soy sauce (1 tablespoon)
1	egg

1. Fill a 2-quart saucepan halfway with water. Bring to a boil.
2. Add frozen vegies and return to a boil.
3. Add the raw ramen. Prepare noodles as directed, reserving seasoning packet. When noodles are tender, drain completely.
4. Place noodles, vegetables, seasoning packet, and soy sauce back into saucepan over medium heat.
5. Crack egg over the mixture, stirring vigorously, until egg is thoroughly cooked.

Yield: 1 serving

RAMEN PRIMAVERA

1/3	cup chopped broccoli
1/3	cup carrots, julienned
1/3	cup red peppers, julienned
1	package Top Ramen or Top Ramen Low Fat, broken into 4 pieces (vegetable flavor)
1	tablespoon olive oil

1. Fill a 2-quart saucepan with 3 cups water and bring to a boil.
2. Add broccoli and carrots to water; cook for 3 minutes.
3. Add the peppers and raw noodles; cook for an additional 3 minutes.
4. Drain mixture; toss with oil and seasoning packet.

Yield: 1 serving

CREAMY RAMEN PRIMAVERA

2	packages Top Ramen or Top Ramen Low Fat (chicken or vegetable flavor)
1	cup frozen chopped broccoli
1	carrot, julienned
1/2	can condensed cream of broccoli soup
3	tablespoons water
1/4	cup grated Parmesan cheese
1/4	teaspoon each pepper and garlic powder

1. Prepare noodles as directed. Drain.
2. In a saucepan boil the broccoli and carrots for 3 minutes.
3. Drain vegies and return to pan. Add soup, water, cheese, and spices. Blend well over low heat.
4. Pour mixture over ramen.

Yield: 2 servings

PRIMAVERA IN TOMATO SAUCE

2	packages Top Ramen or Top Ramen Low Fat (any flavor)
1	tablespoon olive oil
1	clove garlic, minced
1/4	cup diced onion
1/2	cup sliced zucchini
1/2	cup finely sliced red bell pepper
1/2	cup sliced yellow squash
2	plum tomatoes, diced
1/2	cup tomato paste
1/4	cup water
1/4	teaspoon pepper
1/2	teaspoon dried basil, crushed
2	tablespoons sliced black olives (garnish)

1. Prepare noodles as directed. Drain.
2. Heat olive oil in a large skillet. Sauté garlic, onion, zucchini, bell pepper, squash, and plum tomatoes for 5 minutes, stirring frequently.
3. Mix tomato paste, water, pepper, and basil. Add to vegies and simmer for 2 minutes.
4. Serve over ramen. Garnish with olive slices.

Yield: 2 servings

RAMENRONI AND CHEESE

2   packages Top Ramen or Top Ramen Low Fat (1 chicken flavor)

1/2   can condensed cheddar cheese soup

1/4   can milk

1/2   teaspoon pepper

1. Prepare noodles as directed. Drain.
2. Whisk together soup, milk, and pepper.
3. Pour over ramen and mix well.

Yield: 2 serving

RAMEN AND THREE CHEESES

1/3   cup shredded mozzarella
1/3   cup ricotta
1/3   cup shredded muenster
3   tablespoons milk
2   packages Top Ramen or Top Ramen
       Low Fat (any flavor)
       Salt and pepper to taste

1. Slowly melt cheeses and milk over low heat, stirring constantly.
2. Prepare noodles as directed. Drain.
3. Stir noodles into melted cheese. Add salt and pepper.

Yield: 2 servings

RAMEN
ALFREDO

2　　packages Top Ramen or Top Ramen
　　　Low Fat (no seasoning packet)
1　　cup light or whipping cream (room
　　　temperature)
1/2　cup grated Parmesan cheese
2　　tablespoons butter
　　　Ground pepper and nutmeg to taste

1. Prepare noodles as directed. Drain. Return noodles to
　 hot pan.
2. Add mixture of cream, cheese, and butter. Toss until
　 coated.
3. Sprinkle top with pepper and nutmeg.

Yield: 2 servings

RAMEN STARCH MEDLEY

2   packages Top Ramen or Top Ramen
       Low Fat noodles (chicken flavor)
2   tablespoons butter
2   cups cooked potatoes, julienned
1   can (16 1/2 ounces) creamed corn
       Pepper to taste

1. Coarsely break ramen and boil for 3 minutes with seasoning packets in the water. Drain.

2. Place noodles into large skillet with potatoes and corn.
   Heat until warmed through.

3. Pepper to taste.

Yield: 3 servings

NOODLE, POTATO, AND VEGETABLE MIX

1	package Top Ramen or Top Ramen Low Fat, coarsely broken (chicken flavor)
1	cup cooked, cubed potato
1	cup mixed vegetables
1	cup milk
	Garlic and chili powder to taste
3	tablespoons grated Parmesan cheese

1. Prepare noodles as directed. Drain.
2. Place all ingredients except cheese in a saucepan. Cook on medium heat, stirring occasionally, until vegetables are soft.
3. Sprinkle with cheese and serve.

Yield: 2 servings

INDIAN RAMEN

1   package Top Ramen or Top Ramen
       Low Fat, coarsely broken (no seasoning
       packet)

1/2   cup chopped, mixed frozen vegetables

2   tablespoons butter

1/4   teaspoon cumin

1/4   teaspoon coriander

1/4   teaspoon chili powder

1. Prepare noodles as directed. Drain.

2. Boil vegies according to package instructions and drain.

3. In a bowl, mix noodles, vegies, butter, and spices.

4. Toss to coat.

Yield: 2 servings

RAMEN WITH CANNELINI BEANS

1	package Top Ramen or Top Ramen Low Fat (no seasoning packet)
1	tablespoon olive oil
1	clove garlic, minced
1	small green pepper, chopped
1/3	cup chopped onion
1/3	cup chopped celery
1/2	cup tomato paste
1/2	cup water
1/4	teaspoon black pepper
	Pinch of parsley
1	cup canned cannelini beans

1. Prepare noodles as directed. Drain.
2. Sauté garlic, green pepper, onion, and celery in oil until limp.
3. Add tomato paste and water; blend thoroughly.
4. Add pepper and parsley; cook on low heat for 15 minutes.
5. Add beans to mixture and cook 5 more minutes.
6. Serve tossed with ramen.

Yield: 2 servings

CHICK PEA AND RAMEN BAKE

2	tablespoons olive oil
2	onions, coarsely chopped
1/4	teaspoon each of salt, pepper, garlic powder, and chili powder
1	can (12 ounces) tomatoes, drained
2	cans chick peas, drained
1	can (8 ounces) sliced water chestnuts, drained
2	packages Top Ramen or Top Ramen Low Fat, coarsely broken (no seasoning packet)
1/4	cup shredded cheddar cheese

1. Sauté the onions and spices in the oil until tender.

2. Stir in tomatoes and simmer (covered) for 10 minutes.

3. Blend in beans, water chestnuts, and broken raw ramen.

4. Pour into a nonstick casserole dish and cover with cheese.

5. Bake (uncovered) at 350°F for 30 minutes.

Yield: 4 servings

VEGETARIAN RAMEN LASAGNA

3	packages Top Ramen or Top Ramen Low Fat (no seasoning packet)
1/2	cup finely chopped zucchini
1/2	cup finely chopped spinach
1/2	cup carrots, julienned
2	cups vegetable-flavored spaghetti sauce
1	egg, beaten
1/2	cup cottage cheese
1/3	cup grated Parmesan cheese
1	pack (6 ounces) sliced mozzarella

1. Prepare noodles as directed. Drain.

2. In a saucepan boil the zucchini, spinach, and carrots until soft; drain. Stir in spaghetti sauce.

3. In a bowl mix the egg, cottage cheese, and half of the Parmesan.

4. In a nonstick baking dish layer half each of the noodles, cottage cheese mixture, and vegie sauce. Then top with half of the mozzarella slices. Repeat and sprinkle the top with the remaining Parmesan.

5. Bake (covered in foil) at 375°F for 30 minutes, or until heated through.
6. Uncover and bake 5 minutes more, until cheese is browned.
7. Let stand 10 minutes before cutting.

Yield: 4 servings

THREE-LAYER RAMEN PIE

3	packages Top Ramen or Top Ramen Low Fat, broken into four pieces (no seasoning packet)
1/3	cup finely chopped onion
3	cloves garlic, minced
1	tablespoon olive oil
1	cup grated Parmesan cheese
3	eggs
1	container (16 ounces) cottage cheese
1	package (10 ounces) frozen chopped spinach, thawed and drained
1/2	teaspoon salt
3	cups spaghetti sauce, divided

1. Prepare noodles as directed. Drain.
2. Sauté onion and garlic in oil until onions are translucent; remove from heat.
3. Add cooked noodles, 1/2 cup of the Parmesan, and 1 of the eggs to onion mixture; mix well.
4. Press mixture into greased baking dish.
5. Combine 2 egg yolks (reserve whites), cottage cheese, spinach, salt, and remaining Parmesan. Spread over pasta layer.

6. In a small bowl, beat 2 egg whites until stiff; fold in 1 1/2 cups of the spaghetti sauce. Pour over spinach mixture.

7. Bake at 350°F for 50–60 minutes. Let stand 10 minutes before serving.

8. Heat remaining spaghetti sauce to serve over pie slices.

Yield: 6 servings

VEGETARIAN STUFFED PEPPERS

2	large green bell peppers
1	package Top Ramen or Top Ramen Low Fat, finely crushed (no seasoning packet)
1	egg
1	cup spaghetti sauce
2	tablespoons grated Parmesan cheese

1. To make pepper shells, cut off tops of peppers and pull out the insides, leaving hollow shells.

2. Prepare noodles as directed. Drain.

3. Mix noodles, egg, and sauce together.

4. Stuff mixture into peppers. Top each pepper with 1 tablespoon of the grated Parmesan cheese.

5. Bake at 375°F for 10–20 minutes or until heated through.

Yield: 2 servings

ASPARAGUS RAMEN WITH LEMON CREAM SAUCE

2	packages Top Ramen or Top Ramen Low Fat (any flavor)
1	pound asparagus, cut into 1-inch pieces
1/2	cup milk
3	ounces cream cheese
1/4	cup butter
1	tablespoon lemon juice
1/2	cup grated Parmesan cheese
1/4	teaspoon pepper

1. Prepare noodles as directed. Drain.
2. In a large pot of boiling water, blanch asparagus pieces for 3 minutes. Drain and set aside.
3. In a skillet, combine milk, cream cheese, butter, and lemon juice. Whisk until warm and blended, about 4–5 minutes.
4. Stir in Parmesan and pepper; toss with ramen and asparagus.

Yield: 3 servings

CABBAGE STRUDEL

1	small head cabbage, shredded (about 3 cups)
1	teaspoon salt
1	teaspoon pepper
1/4	cup butter, softened
1	package commercial pie shell mix
1/4	cup sour cream
1	package Top Ramen or Top Ramen Low Fat, crushed (no seasoning packet)

1. Mix shredded cabbage and spices. Sauté with most of the butter for 15 minutes. Take off heat.

2. Meanwhile prepare pie shell mix and roll out into a rectangle.* (Be sure to sprinkle a little flour onto your rolling surface to make sure the dough doesn't stick.)

3. Gently spread sour cream, cabbage, and raw ramen onto shell to within 1/2 inch of the sides. Fold the uneven parts of the 4 sides in. Roll up the rectangle of dough and filling from one end of the rectangle to the other.

4. Cut in half and place in a covered nonstick baking dish. Baste top of strudel with remaining butter.

5. Bake at 350°F for 35–45 minutes. Cut into rolls and serve.

*Use a plastic liter soda bottle if you don't own a rolling pin.

Yield: 4 servings

ENTREES WITH BEEF AND PORK

We have included many recipes with ground beef because it is an easy ingredient to use. Feel free, however, to substitute tofu or textured vegetable protein for beef in any of the following recipes. Also, when browning ground beef, we do not recommend using butter or oil because even the leanest ground beef has enough grease to brown itself.

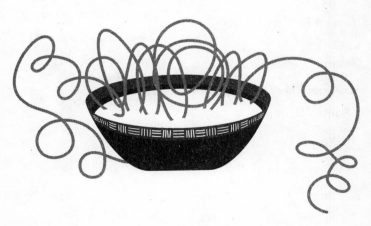

BEEFY
RAMEN

1   package Top Ramen or Top Ramen
       Low Fat (beef flavor)
2   tablespoons Worcestershire sauce
3   slices American cheese

1. Prepare noodles as directed. Don't drain.

2. Add Worcestershire sauce and stir.

3. Lay cheese on top of ramen. Cover and remove from heat.

4. When cheese has melted, stir again.

Yield: 1 serving

RAMEN
CHILI

3   packages Top Ramen or Top Ramen
    Low Fat, coarsely broken (2 beef
    flavor packets)
2   tablespoons butter
1/3 cup chopped onion
1   teaspoon chili powder
1   can (15 ounces) commercial chili
2   tablespoons jalapeno pepper slices
1/2 cup sour cream
1   tablespoon chopped cilantro

1. Prepare noodles as directed, reserving seasoning packets. Drain.

2. Sauté onion in butter. Add chili powder and the two seasoning packets to onions; stir.

3. Add chili and ramen to onion mixture and stir over low heat until warmed through. Add jalapeno, sour cream, and cilantro to top before serving.

≈**NOTE**≈ A nice variation is to add 2/3 cup processed cheese spread to skillet when combining chili and ramen. Stir until cheese is melted.

Yield: 4 servings

SWEET AND SOUR HOT DOGS

 2   hot dogs, sliced
 1   package Top Ramen or Top Ramen
       Low Fat (pork flavor)
 1   packet each Chinese hot mustard, duck
       sauce, and soy sauce (1 tablespoon each)

1. Fill a 2-quart saucepan halfway with water and bring to a boil. Add hot dogs. Cook 2 minutes.

2. Add raw ramen and seaoning packet and boil 3 more minutes. Drain.

3. Add sauces to noodles and hot dogs; toss to coat.

Yield: 1 serving

SKILLET FRANKS
AND NOODLES

2   hot dogs, sliced
1   package Top Ramen or Top Ramen
      Low Fat, crushed (pork flavor)
1   tablespoon ketchup
1   tablespoon mustard
      Salt and pepper to taste

1. Fill a 2-quart saucepan halfway with water and boil. Add hot dogs and boil for 3 minutes.

2. Add raw noodles and seasoning packet and boil for 3 more minutes. Drain.

3. Add ketchup, mustard, salt, and pepper. Stir.

≈**NOTE**≈ You might like to add 2 slices American cheese or 1/2 cup canned chili to top of mixture before serving.

Yield: 1 serving

TOMATO HOT DOGS AND NOODLES

1	package Top Ramen or Top Ramen Low Fat, coarsely broken (pork flavor)
1	hot dog
2/3	cup stewed tomatoes
1/4	teaspoon onion flakes

1. Prepare noodles as directed. Drain.
2. Boil hot dog and slice into thin strips. Mix all ingredients and heat through.

Yield: 1 serving

ORIENTAL SAUSAGE RAMEN

1   package Top Ramen or Top Ramen Low Fat (pork flavor)

$1/2$ cup sliced summer sausage

1   packet soy sauce (1 tablespoon)

1. Prepare noodles as directed. Drain.
2. Brown sausage in soy sauce.
3. Add noodles and cook for 2 minutes on low heat.

Yield: 1 serving

DIJON SAUSAGE RAMEN

    1/4   pound sliced kielbasa
    1   package Top Ramen or Top Ramen
              Low Fat (pork flavor)
    1   teaspoon Dijon mustard
    1   packet soy sauce (1 tablespoon)

1. Fry kielbasa.
2. Prepare noodles as directed but do not drain.
3. Stir kielbasa, mustard, and soy sauce into ramen. Heat through.

Yield: 1 serving

CREAMY MUSHROOM AND BEEF RAMEN

2   packages Top Ramen or Top Ramen Low Fat, broken into 4 pieces (beef flavor)
1/3   pound ground beef
1/4   cup water
1/2   can condensed cream of mushroom soup

1. Prepare noodles as directed, reserving seasoning packet. Drain.
2. In a medium fry pan, brown ground beef. Drain fat if desired.
3. Add mixture of water and cream of mushroom soup; blend well. Reduce heat to lowest setting.
4. Add ramen and seasoning packets to beef and soup mixture. Stir for two minutes and serve.

Yield: 2 servings

RAMEN CARBONARA

1	package Top Ramen or Top Ramen Low Fat (pork flavor)
1	tablespoon butter
2	ounces ($1/8$ cup) grated Parmesan cheese
2	tablespoons milk or cream
$1/4$	cup cooked ham or lunchmeat, chopped

1. Prepare noodles as directed. Drain.
2. In a small saucepan, melt butter and stir in Parmesan and milk. Stir in ham or lunchmeat and heat through.
3. Toss noodles with cream mixture.

Yield: 1 serving

PORK AND BEANS RAMEN

1	package Top Ramen or Top Ramen Low Fat, coarsely broken (any flavor)
1	sliced hot dog
1	can (12–16 ounces) pork and beans
1/2	teaspoon chili powder (optional)
1	tablespoon honey (optional)

1. In a large saucepan, prepare noodles as directed, boiling hot dog with noodles and seasoning packet. Drain and return to pan.

2. Stir can of pork and beans into noodles and hot dogs. Mix well and heat through.

3. Add optional ingredients if desired.

Yield: 2 servings

ITALIAN RAMEN CASSEROLE

2   packages Top Ramen or Top Ramen Low Fat (beef flavor)

1/2   pound ground beef, browned

2   cups any flavor spaghetti sauce

4   slices mozzarella cheese

1. Prepare noodles as directed. Drain and place noodles in the bottom of a nonstick casserole dish.

2. Cover the noodles with browned ground meat. Pour the sauce over the meat and noodles. Top with layer of cheese slices.

3. Bake (uncovered) at 350°F for 25 minutes, until cheese is melted.

Yield: 2 servings

SPICY NUTTY PORK RAMEN

1	package Top Ramen or Top Ramen Low Fat (pork flavor)
1	tablespoon peanut oil
1	clove garlic, finely chopped
1/4	cup chopped scallions
	Dash red pepper flakes
1	packet soy sauce (1 tablespoon)
1	tablespoon peanut butter
1	teaspoon rice vinegar
1/2	teaspoon sugar
1/4	teaspoon sesame oil
1/2	cup cubed, cooked pork

1. Prepare noodles as directed. Drain.
2. In a wok, heat the peanut oil and sauté the garlic and scallions for 2 minutes.
3. Reduce heat and add the rest of the ingredients. Stir-fry the mixture until heated through.

Yield: 2 servings

RAMEN STROGANOFF

1	package Top Ramen or Top Ramen Low Fat (beef flavor)
1/4	pound ground beef
1/2	cup fresh, sliced mushrooms
1/3	cup minced onion
1/2	cup sour cream
1	tablespoon flour

1. Prepare noodles as directed. Drain.

2. In a large skillet cook meat, mushrooms, and onion. Drain grease.

3. Mix sour cream and flour; pour over the meat mixture in skillet. Cook over low heat until bubbly.

4. Pour over ramen and toss to coat.

Yield: 1 serving

BEEF
LO-MEIN

2   cups cooked ground beef
1   tablespoon peanut oil
1   medium carrot, finely chopped
1/4 cup chopped scallions
1   teaspoon garlic powder
3   packets soy sauce (3 tablespoons)
1   package Top Ramen or Top Ramen
     Low Fat, coarsely broken (beef or
     oriental flavor)

1. In a 10-inch skillet, brown ground beef. Drain fat. Remove to a warm platter.

2. In same skillet, heat oil and sauté carrots, scallions, and garlic powder until carrots are still somewhat crisp.

3. Add beef and soy sauce and stir to coat.

4. Prepare noodles as directed. Drain.

5. Combine all ingredients in skillet and sauté for 1 minute.

≈**NOTE**≈ Interesting variations are to substitute pork for the beef to make pork lo-mein, or substitute 1 cup chopped broccoli for the beef (with 1/3 cup each of water chestnuts and chopped celery) to make vegetable lo-mein.

Yield: 2 servings

RAMEN BEEF AND VEGIE SKILLET

1	tablespoon butter
6	ounces ground beef
1	medium yellow onion, chopped
1	can (8 ounces) chopped tomatoes (with juice)
1	stalk celery, finely chopped
$1/2$	teaspoon salt
$1/4$	teaspoon black pepper
$1/4$	teaspoon each basil and oregano
1	package Top Ramen or Top Ramen Low Fat, coarsely broken (beef flavor)

1. Melt the butter in a skillet over medium heat until bubbly.
2. Add the beef and onion. Cook uncovered, stirring occasionally, until beef is brown and onion is limp.
3. Add the tomatoes, celery, spices, raw ramen and seasoning packet.
4. Cover and simmer 20 minutes, stirring occasionally until noodles are soft.

Yield: 2 servings

GROUND BEEF
STIR-FRY

1/2	pound ground beef
3	packets soy sauce (3 tablespoons)
1/2	teaspoon celery salt
1	cup chopped broccoli
1	cup chopped cauliflower
1	small onion, coarsely chopped
1/2	red bell pepper, cut into strips
2	packages Top Ramen or Top Ramen Low Fat (any flavor)

1. In a wok, brown ground meat in soy sauce and celery salt.
2. Add vegetables and stir-fry until vegetables are still a bit crisp.
3. Prepare noodles as directed. Drain.
4. Serve the stir-fry over noodles.

Yield: 3 servings

CABBAGE AND BEEF SKILLET

2	packages Top Ramen or Top Ramen Low Fat (beef flavor)
1/2	pound ground beef
1	egg, beaten
1/2	cup finely chopped onion
1/4	cup chopped green pepper
1	clove garlic, minced
1/2	tablespoon parsley
1	tablespoon vegetable oil
1/2	medium head cabbage, shredded (about 2 cups)
2	tablespoons water

1. Prepare noodles as directed with only one seasoning packet. Drain.

2. In a bowl, mix ground beef, egg, onion, green pepper, garlic, parsley, and second seasoning packet.

3. In a large fry pan heat oil. Add beef mixture and brown, stirring frequently.

4. Add cabbage and water. Reduce heat and cook (covered) for approximately 15 minutes, stirring occasionally. Serve the mixture over ramen.

≈**NOTE**≈ For a sweet and sour variation, add 3 packets each of duck sauce and hot mustard into the mixture.

RAMEN MEATLOAF

1	package Top Ramen or Top Ramen Low Fat, crushed (beef flavor)
1	pound ground beef
1	egg
1	small onion, minced
1/4	teaspoon salt
	Dash pepper
	Splash Worcestershire sauce (optional)
	Dash oregano

1. Preheat oven to 350°F.

2. Prepare noodles as directed. Drain.

3. In a medium bowl, combine noodles with all other ingredients except oregano and mix thoroughly.

4. Transfer the mixture to shallow baking dish and shape into a loaf.

5. Sprinkle oregano over top.

6. Bake uncovered for 60 minutes. (Keep checking to make sure loaf is not too dry; if you need to, add a cover.)

7. Cut into slices and serve.

Yield: 4 servings

SURPRISE RAMEN MEATLOAF

2	pounds ground beef
1	small onion, minced
2	eggs, beaten
1	package Top Ramen or Top Ramen Low Fat, crushed (beef flavor)
1	cup tomato sauce
	Salt and pepper to taste

1. Mix meat, seasoning packet, onion, and eggs.

2. Cover the bottom of a small baking pan with half of the beef mixture.

3. Form a well in the middle of the mixture and place the raw ramen and tomato sauce in the center.

4. Cover with remaining meat and bake uncovered at 350°F for 60 minutes.

Yield: 4 servings

CHEESEBURGER NOODLES

1/4	pound ground beef
1	package Top Ramen or Top Ramen Low Fat, crushed (beef flavor)
2	slices American cheese (each piece broken into 4)
1	tablespoon ketchup
1	tablespoon mustard
	Salt and pepper to taste
2	tomato slices

1. In a fry pan, brown the ground beef and drain.
2. Prepare noodles as directed. Drain.
3. Mix the beef and noodles in a saucepan over low to medium heat. Lay the cheese on top of the mixture and cover for approximately 3 minutes until cheese is melted.
4. Stir the mixture, adding ketchup, mustard, salt, and pepper.
5. Garnish with slices of tomato.

Yield: 1 serving

CALIFORNIA BEEF OVER RAMEN

2	packages Top Ramen or Top Ramen Low Fat (beef flavor)
1	pound ground beef
1	small onion, chopped
1/4	teaspoon pepper
1	clove garlic, minced
1	can condensed cream of mushroom soup
3/4	cup plain yogurt
1	avocado, cubed

1. Prepare noodles as directed, reserving seasoning packet. Drain.
2. Brown meat in a fry pan.
3. Add onion, seasoning packet, pepper, and garlic. Stir and cook until onion is translucent.
4. Blend in soup. (You may add a little water if mixture is too thick.)
5. Fold in yogurt and avocado; heat for 3 minutes. Serve over ramen.

Yield: 4 servings

SHANGHAI PORK
SURPRISE

1	tablespoon peanut oil
1	clove garlic, minced
1/4	cup chopped scallions
1/2	cup chopped broccoli
1/2	cup chopped carrots
1/2	cup snow peas, tips and strings removed
1/2	cup cooked, cubed pork
2	packets soy sauce (2 tablespoons)
1	package Top Ramen or Top Ramen Low Fat (pork flavor)

1. In a wok, heat peanut oil and sauté garlic and scallions for 2 minutes.

2. Add broccoli, carrots, snow peas; stir-fry for 3 minutes.

3. Add pork and soy sauce; stir to coat.

4. Prepare noodles as directed. Drain.

5. Serve the stir-fry over noodles.

Yield: 2 servings

RAMEN WITH GREEN BEANS, MUSHROOMS, AND BACON

2	packages Top Ramen or Top Ramen Low Fat, broken into 4 pieces (mushroom or pork flavor)
1	package (10 ounces) frozen French-cut green beans
6	slices bacon
1	can condensed cream of mushroom soup
1/2	cup milk
1	small can (6 ounces) sliced, drained mushrooms

1. Prepare 1 1/2 packages of the ramen with seasoning packets. Drain.

2. Cook green beans according to package directions; drain.

3. Fry bacon; drain on paper towels and crumble.

4. Mix cooked noodles, green beans, soup, milk, and mushrooms in a medium nonstick casserole dish. Top with bacon.

5. Cover and bake at 350°F for 20 minutes or until bubbly.

6. Crush the remaining uncooked ramen and top the dish with it; bake 5 minutes more.

RAMEN
NOODLE PIE

1	package Top Ramen or Top Ramen Low Fat (beef flavor)
2	tablespoons butter, melted
2	tablespoons grated Parmesan cheese
2	eggs, beaten
1	cup cottage cheese
1/3	pound ground beef
1/4	cup chopped onion
1/2	cup diced green pepper
1	can (8 ounces) stewed tomatoes
1/2	cup tomato paste
1/4	teaspoon sugar
1/4	teaspoon oregano
1/4	teaspoon garlic powder
6	ounces shredded mozzarella cheese

1. Prepare noodles as directed reserving the seasoning packet. Drain.
2. Stir noodles, butter, Parmesan, and eggs together in a medium saucepan.
3. Press mixture into bottom of greased pie pan.
4. Spread cottage cheese over noodle mixture.
5. Brown meat.

6. Stir in onion, green pepper, stewed tomatoes (with liquid), tomato paste, sugar, oregano, garlic powder, and seasoning packet.

7. Spread the meat mixture over the cottage cheese.

8. Bake at 350°F for 15–20 minutes. Sprinkle top with mozzarella and cook 5 more minutes.

Yield: 2 servings

SOUR CREAM NOODLE BAKE

2   packages Top Ramen or Top Ramen Low Fat noodles (beef flavor)
1/2   cup chopped green onions
1/2   pound ground beef
1/4   teaspoon each black pepper and garlic salt
1   cup sour cream
1/2   cup shredded mozzarella cheese

1. Prepare noodles as directed using one seasoning packet. Drain and mix noodles with green onions. Set aside.

2. In a 10-inch skillet, brown ground beef; drain fat. Add second seasoning packet, pepper, garlic salt, and sour cream; blend well.

3. Alternate layers of noodle mixture and meat sauce in a greased casserole, beginning with noodles and ending with meat. Top with mozzarella.

4. Bake (uncovered) at 350°F for 20 minutes, until cheese is brown.

Yield: 3 servings

RAMEN AND MEATBALLS WITH CELERY

1/2	pound ground beef
1/4	cup quick-cook oats
	Pinch each salt and pepper
1/2	seasoning packet (beef flavor)
1 1/2	tablespoons butter
1	package Top Ramen or Top Ramen Low Fat, coarsely broken
1	cup celery, sliced
1/2	onion, chopped
1	can condensed cream of celery soup
1	cup water

1. Mix the ground beef, oats, and spices; form into balls and sauté in butter and half of the seasoning packet.

2. Arrange half of the meatballs in the bottom of a greased casserole dish. Add the raw ramen, celery, and onion. Top with other half of meatballs.

3. Mix soup and water and pour over rest of ingredients.

4. Bake (covered) at 350°F for 50 minutes.

Yield: 4 servings

RAMEN
LASAGNA

1/2	pound ground beef
1/4	cup chopped onion
3	cups spaghetti sauce
2	packages Top Ramen or Top Ramen Low Fat (beef flavor)
1	pound ricotta cheese
1	egg
2	tablespoons chopped fresh parsley
1/4	teaspoon each salt and pepper
4	ounces shredded mozzarella cheese Grated Parmesan cheese (for topping)

1. Brown ground beef and onion in a large saucepan.

2. Add spaghetti sauce; bring to a boil and reduce heat.

3. Simmer 15 minutes.

4. Prepare noodles as directed. Drain.

5. In a bowl combine ricotta, egg, parsley, salt, and pepper.

6. In a nonstick baking pan layer as follows: 1/2 of the meat sauce, noodles, and ricotta mixture, ending with remaining meat sauce and mozzarella.

7. Sprinkle top with Parmesan and cover with foil.

8. Bake at 375°F for 25–30 minutes.

9. Remove foil and bake approximately 5 minutes longer until cheese is browned.

Yield: 4 servings

ICE STORM CASSEROLE

1/2   pound ground beef
4   small to medium raw potatoes, sliced
1   small onion, sliced
1 1/2   packages Top Ramen or Top Ramen
         Low Fat, coarsely broken (beef flavor)
1   can condensed cheddar cheese soup
1/2   can water

1. Brown ground meat with one seasoning packet.
2. Grease a casserole pan and layer potatoes, meat, onions, and 1 package of raw ramen; repeat.
3. Top layers with crushed remaining raw ramen. Then pour combined soup and water evenly over top of casserole.
4. Bake covered at 375°F for 55 minutes.
5. Bake for another 15 minutes uncovered.

≈**NOTE**≈ For a tangy variation, add 1/3 cup tomato paste and a dash of Tabasco sauce to the soup mixture before pouring over casserole ingredients.

Yield: 4 servings

SAUSAGE CASSEROLE

2   packages Top Ramen or Top Ramen Low Fat (pork flavor)
1   tablespoon butter
$1/2$ cup chopped onion
$1/2$ cup chopped celery
1   can (16 ounces) creamed corn
$1/2$ cup sour cream
$1/2$ teaspoon salt
    Dash pepper
$1/2$ pound smoked kielbasa, sliced

1. Prepare noodles as directed. Drain.
2. Sauté onion and celery in butter until tender; remove from heat.
3. Add noodles, corn, sour cream, salt, and pepper to the onions and celery and transfer all into a shallow nonstick baking dish.
4. Arrange the sliced sausage on top of mixture.
5. Bake at 350°F for 35–40 minutes.

Yield: 4 servings

BEEF, VEGIE, AND NOODLE CASSEROLE

1	pound ground beef
1	medium onion, chopped
1/2	teaspoon seasoned salt
1/2	teaspoon oregano
1/2	teaspoon basil
1/2	teaspoon garlic powder
1	cup chopped zucchini
2	carrots, sliced
2	packages Top Ramen or Top Ramen Low Fat, coarsely broken (any flavor)
1	can condensed cream of mushroom soup
1	cup water
6	slices American cheese

1. Sauté meat, onion, and spices in large fry pan.
2. Boil zucchini, carrots, and ramen in saucepan for 3 minutes with the flavor packets in the water. Drain.
3. Mix all ingredients but the cheese into a greased casserole.
4. Top mixture with a layer of cheese.
5. Bake uncovered at 350°F for 30 minutes.

Yield: 4 servings

HUNGARIAN PEPPERDISH

4	large red bell peppers
1	pound ground beef
1	onion, chopped
1	tomato, chopped
2	cloves garlic, minced
1	teaspoon paprika
1	package Top Ramen or Top Ramen Low Fat, crushed (beef flavor)
1/4	cup grated cheese
1 1/4	cups water
	Sour cream (optional)

1. Clean the peppers, cut off the tops, and remove the insides.

2. Mix the rest of the ingredients except water and cheese.

3. Fill the peppers with the mixture; sprinkle the tops with cheese.

4. Put the peppers in a baking dish, pouring the water in the bottom to prevent burning.

5. Bake at 350°F for 30 minutes.

6. Serve with sour cream.

Yield: 4 servings

STEAK AND RAMEN

3   tablespoons oil, divided
3/4   pound flank steak, cut into strips
       (or ground beef)
2   medium zucchini, cut in 1/2-inch slices
11/2 cup fresh, sliced mushrooms
2   small onions, coarsely chopped
1   cup warm water
1   tablespoon flour
1/4   red wine vinegar
2   teaspoons sugar
3   packages Top Ramen or Top Ramen
       Low Fat, broken into 4 pieces, (beef flavor)

1. In a large skillet heat 1 tablespoon of the oil and cook beef strips. Remove to a bowl.

2. In the warm skillet place remaining oil and sauté zucchini, mushrooms, and onions until tender.

3. In a small bowl, combine the warm water, seasoning packets, and flour and stir.

4. Add water mixture, vinegar, and sugar to vegies in skillet.

5. Heat the vegetable mixture to a boil (boil for 1 minute).
6. Prepare noodles as directed. Drain.
7. Mix vegetables, meat, and noodles.

Yield: 4 servings

HOMEMADE GOULASH OVER RAMEN

1/2	cup flour
	Dash each salt and pepper
2	tablespoons oil
1	pound stew meat, cubed
2	tablespoons butter
3	tablespoons flour
2	cups water
2	packages Top Ramen or Top Ramen Low Fat (beef flavor)

1. Place the flour, salt, and pepper in a sealable plastic bag. Put the meat in the bag and shake to coat with flour mixture.

2. In oil, sear the meat on all sides in a hot fry pan.

3. Put the meat in a nonstick baking dish.

4. Add the butter and flour to the fry pan used for the meat. Stir until flour has absorbed the butter.

5. Slowly add the water and seasoning packets, whisking constantly. Bring the sauce to a boil, stirring constantly; then pour over meat.

6. Cover and bake at 350°F for 75 minutes.
7. Prepare noodles as directed. Drain.
8. Serve over noodles.

Yield: 4 servings

STUFFED CABBAGE

"Party Meatballs" mix (see page 14)
1   large head cabbage (about 5 cups)
1   jar (24 ounces) sauerkraut or 2 cups (optional)
    Sour cream (optional)

1. For the filling, use the recipe for "Party Meatballs." Do not cook.

2. Core the head of cabbage. Holding it under running water, carefully separate and remove about 14 leaves.

3. Blanch the leaves by dipping them 3 at a time in boiling water (about 3 minutes) then cool.

4. Place 3–4 teaspoons of uncooked Party Meatball mixture at the base of each leaf. Roll leaf toward top, then fold sides under—creating a pillow shape.

5. Pack the rolls into a small, greased baking pan.

6. Bake (uncovered) at 350°F for 30 minutes.

7. Serve with either sour cream or heated sauerkraut.

Yield: 4 servings

ENTREES WITH FISH AND POULTRY

As with the beef and pork entrees, feel free to substitute tofu or textured vegetable protein for fish and poultry in the following recipes.

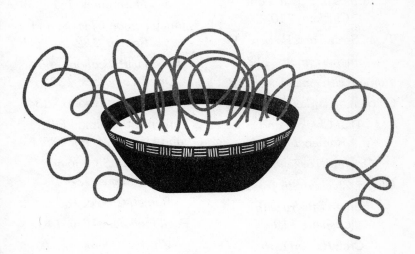

FRIED RAMEN WITH CHICKEN SALAD

1   package Top Ramen or Top Ramen
Low Fat (chicken flavor)
1   cup chicken salad (canned or fresh)

1. Prepare noodles as directed. Drain.
2. Prepare "Fried Ramen" (see page 31) by pressing noodles into small skillet and cooking until crisp on the bottom.
3. Spread chicken salad on top, being careful not to get the salad too close to the edge of the noodles.
4. When noodles are sufficiently brown on bottom and chicken salad is warmed through, cut into pie-shaped wedges and serve.

Yield: 1 serving

RAMEN WITH SHRIMP IN GARLIC BUTTER

4	tablespoons butter
1/4	pound shrimp, peeled and deveined
1	clove garlic, minced
1	package Top Ramen or Top Ramen Low Fat (no seasoning packet)
	Coarsely ground black pepper (for garnish)

1. Melt butter in medium saucepan. Add shrimp and garlic and cook over moderate heat until shrimp turn pink and become firm.
2. Prepare noodles as directed. Drain.
3. Toss noodles with shrimp mixture.
4. Sprinkle black pepper over noodles before serving.

Yield: 1 serving

TURKEY
TETTRAZINI

2	packages Top Ramen or Top Ramen Low Fat, coarsely broken (chicken flavor)
1	cup cooked, cubed turkey
1/3	cup condensed cream of chicken soup
1/3	cup milk
1/4	teaspoon instant minced onion
2	tablespoons grated cheddar cheese
1/2	teaspoon parsley flakes
	Dash Worcestershire sauce
	Salt and pepper to taste

1. Prepare noodles as directed. Drain.
2. Combine noodles with rest of ingredients; cook over low heat for 10 minutes or until mixture is hot.

Yield: 2 servings

MINCED
MEXICAN CLAMS

1   small (6–8 ounces) can minced clams, drained
1   tablespoon olive oil
2   tablespoons salsa
1   teaspoon dried, crushed oregano
1   package Top Ramen or Top Ramen Low Fat (no seasoning packet)

1. In medium skillet, sauté minced clams in olive oil for about 3 minutes.

2. Add salsa and oregano. Simmer 5 minutes stirring occasionally.

3. Prepare noodles as directed. Drain.

4. Remove clam mixture from heat and toss with noodles.

Yield: 1 serving

CHEESY CHICKEN NOODLE BAKE

        1   tablespoon oil
        1   boneless chicken breast, cut into 2 halves
        2   packages Top Ramen or Top Ramen
                Low Fat (chicken flavor)
        1   can condensed cheddar cheese soup
                Dash each salt and pepper

1. Preheat oven to 400°F.

2. Brown the chicken breasts in oil (about 1 minute on each side); remove from heat.

3. Prepare noodles as directed. Drain.

4. Place noodles in the bottom of a shallow casserole dish. Place chicken breasts on top of noodles. Pour cheese soup over ingredients, completely covering chicken and noodles (don't toss).

5. Season with salt and pepper.

6. Bake uncovered for 30 minutes or until chicken is cooked through. (The cheese may be a little brown on top but not burnt.)

Yield: 2 servings

BAKED RAMEN AND SOUR CREAM CHICKEN

1   container (8 ounces) sour cream
1   pound boneless, skinless chicken breasts
1   package Top Ramen or Top Ramen
      Low Fat, finely crushed (chicken flavor)

1. Mix sour cream and seasoning packet.
2. In a nonstick casserole dish, spread sour cream mixture over chicken breasts.
3. Top with raw noodles.
4. Bake at 350°F for 1 hour.

Yield: 4 servings

CREAMY TUNA AND RAMEN

2	packages Top Ramen or Top Ramen Low Fat (chicken or shrimp flavor)
1	tablespoon butter
1	tablespoon flour
3/4	cup of milk
1	can (6 1/8 ounces) of tuna, drained
	Dash pepper
1/8	teaspoon salt
	Dash onion powder

1. Prepare noodles as directed. Drain.
2. In a 1-quart saucepan melt butter over low heat. Add flour, stirring constantly.
2. When flour has absorbed butter, slowly stir in milk. Continue stirring until mixture begins to thicken.
4. Add tuna, pepper, salt, and onion powder.
5. Pour creamy tuna sauce over ramen and serve.

Yield: 2 servings

CHICKEN À LA KING RAMEN

3	tablespoons butter, melted
3	tablespoons flour
1	cup hot water
1	cup milk
1	cup cooked, cubed chicken or turkey
2	packages Top Ramen or Top Ramen Low Fat (chicken flavor)

1. Stir flour into melted butter until absorbed.

2. Slowly whisk in hot water and milk. Simmer but don't boil.

3. Add chicken or turkey cubes. Stir in seasoning packets and heat through.

4. Prepare noodles as directed. Drain and serve sauce over noodles.

Yield: 2 servings

RAMEN WITH TUNA AND PARSLEY

1	can (6.5 ounces) white tuna packed in water, drained
6	tablespoons olive oil
1	tablespoon lemon juice
1/2	cup chopped fresh parsley
1/4	teaspoon black pepper
1/4	teaspoon salt
2	packages Top Ramen or Top Ramen Low Fat (no seasoning packet)

1. In a small bowl, divide tuna into chunks and add oil.
2. Stir in lemon juice, parsley, pepper, and salt.
3. Prepare noodles as directed. Drain.
4. Toss tuna and parsley mixture with noodles until coated.

Yield: 2 servings

PARMESAN NOODLES AND CHICKEN

2   packages Top Ramen or Top Ramen
     Low Fat, coarsely broken (chicken flavor)
1   can condensed cream of chicken soup
1/2 cup milk
1/3 cup grated Parmesan cheese
     Dash pepper
2   cups cooked, cubed chicken

1. Prepare noodles as directed. Drain.
2. In a medium saucepan over medium heat, combine soup, milk, cheese, and pepper.
3. Add cooked noodles and chicken. Stir until heated through.

Yield: 2 servings

TUNA, SPICES, AND RAMEN

1	package Top Ramen or Top Ramen Low Fat (no seasoning packet)
1	can (6 1/8 ounces) tuna in water, drained
2	tablespoons olive oil
1/2	teaspoon garlic powder
1	teaspoon dried basil
1	tablespoon dried parsley
1	cup milk
2	pinches pepper
1	teaspoon cornstarch
4	tablespoons grated Parmesan cheese

1. Prepare noodles as directed. Drain.
2. Mix rest of ingredients except Parmesan, and then stir in noodles.
3. Sprinkle Parmesan over mixture.

Yield: 2 servings

RAMEN
TONNATO

1	package Top Ramen or Top Ramen Low Fat (no seasoning packet)
3/4	cup commercial Italian salad dressing
2	cans (6¹/₈ ounces) tuna packed in oil, drained
1	can (8 ounces) black, pitted olives
1	jar (4 ounces) roasted red peppers
3	tablespoons capers (optional)

1. Prepare noodles as directed. Drain.
2. Mix with rest of ingredients.

≈**NOTE**≈ For variation, get a crusty loaf of unsliced bread and cut off about an inch on the top (all in one slice). Pick out the insides of the loaf and toss to the birds (or save for another use). Fill the cavity with Tonnato, place the top back on the bread, wrap it tightly in plastic wrap, and chill for four hours. Slice and serve.

Yield: 2 servings

RAMEN WITH ANCHOVIES

1	package Top Ramen or Top Ramen Low Fat (no seasoning packet)
1	tablespoon olive oil
1	clove garlic, finely chopped
	About 4 anchovies, drained and mashed
2	tablespoons bread crumbs

1. Prepare noodles as directed. Drain.
2. In a small skillet, heat olive oil and sauté garlic about 2 minutes.
3. Toss noodles with garlic and anchovies. Sprinkle bread crumbs over top.

Yield: 1 serving

CHICKEN OR TURKEY HASH

1 package Top Ramen or Top Ramen
  Low Fat, finely crushed (chicken flavor)
2 tablespoons butter
1/2 small onion, chopped
1 cup cooked, cubed chicken or turkey
1 cup cooked, cubed potatoes
  Dash chili powder

1. Prepare noodles as directed. Drain but leave about 1 tablespoon water in bottom.

2. In a 10-inch skillet over high heat, sauté onion in butter until translucent.

3. Add chicken and potatoes; reduce heat. Stir mixture until warmed through.

4. Add moist noodles and stir in chili powder. Salt and pepper to taste.

Yield: 2 servings

THAI CHICKEN AND RAMEN

1	package Top Ramen or Top Ramen Low Fat (chicken flavor)
1	cup cooked chicken, thinly sliced
1	medium cucumber, thinly shredded
1/2	cup shredded cooked ham
1	tablespoon toasted sesame seeds

Sauce:

3	packets soy sauce (3 tablespoons)
1 1/2	tablespoons vinegar
1	teaspoon sugar
3/4	teaspoon Tabasco sauce
3	tablespoons chopped green onion
1 1/2	tablespoons sesame oil
1/2	cup water

1. Prepare noodles as directed. Drain.
2. Mix sauce ingredients in a bowl and set aside.
3. To serve, place noodles on serving plates. Top with chicken, cucumber, and ham. Pour on the sauce and sprinkle with sesame seeds.

Yield: 2 servings

ORIENTAL TURKEY

2 tablespoons oil, divided
1 turkey tenderloin (medium size), cut into strips
1 carrot, sliced on the bias
1/2 red pepper, julienned
1 clove garlic, minced
1/4 teaspoon fresh minced ginger
1/2 cup orange juice
1 packet soy sauce (1 tablespoon)
1 tablespoon cornstarch
3 tablespoons finely chopped scallions
2 packages Top Ramen or Top Ramen Low Fat (no seasoning packet)

1. In wok, heat 1 tablespoon of the oil until hot and stir-fry turkey strips until lightly browned. Remove turkey to warm platter.

2. Add remaining tablespoon of oil, carrots, red pepper, garlic, and ginger to wok; stir-fry about 3 minutes.

3. In a small bowl, combine orange juice, soy sauce, cornstarch, and scallions; stir until cornstarch is dissolved.

4. Add this mixture to wok and continue to toss ingredients while heating.

5. Return turkey to wok with vegetables and cook until heated through.

6. Prepare noodles as directed. Drain. Serve the stir-fry over noodles.

Yield: 2 servings

GINGER CHICKEN STIR-FRY

2	packages Top Ramen or Top Ramen Low Fat (1 oriental flavor)
2	tablespoons olive oil
1	packet soy sauce (1 tablespoon)
1/2	teaspoon minced ginger
1	clove garlic, minced
3/4	pound boneless chicken breast, cut into strips
1/2	cup chopped broccoli
1	small onion, coarsely chopped
1	yellow bell pepper, chopped
1	tomato, chopped

1. Prepare noodles as directed, reserving seasoning packet. Drain.
2. Mix olive oil, seasoning packet, soy sauce, ginger, and garlic.
3. Pour sauce into heated skillet and brown chicken breast strips on all sides.
4. Add broccoli and onion; sauté for 2 minutes. Add bell pepper and tomato. Heat until all vegies are limp. Serve over ramen.

Yield: 4 servings

RAMEN STIR-FRY WITH CASHEWS

2	tablespoons oil
1/2	boneless chicken breast, cut up (about 1 cup)
1/2	cup broccoli florets
1/2	cup carrots, sliced on the bias
1/4	cup cashews
2	packets soy sauce (2 tablespoons)
1	package Top Ramen or Top Ramen Low Fat (chicken flavor)

1. In a wok or large saucepan, heat oil. Stir-fry chicken chunks until almost cooked through; move to sides of wok.

2. Stir-fry broccoli and carrots until still a bit crisp.

3. Mix chicken with vegetables and stir in cashews and soy sauce. Stir-fry for two more minutes or until heated through.

4. Prepare noodles as directed. Drain. Serve chicken stir-fry over cooked ramen.

Yield: 2 servings

CRAB RAMEN WITH SNOWPEAS

2   tablespoons butter
1   cup crabmeat or imitation crab meat
2   cups snowpeas, tips and strings removed
1   packages Top Ramen or Top Ramen
      Low Fat (no seasoning packet)
Dressing:
1   tablespoon butter
1   teaspoon garlic powder
1   tablespoon flour
1/4   teaspoon dried, crushed oregano
1/8   teaspoon salt
      Dash pepper
3/4   cup milk

1. In a 10-inch skillet, melt butter and sauté crabmeat and snowpeas until peas are tender. Set aside.

2. To make dressing, melt butter in a small saucepan. Stir in garlic powder, flour, oregano, salt, and pepper.

3. Add milk all at once. Cook and stir over medium heat till thick and bubbly. Remove from heat and stir one minute more.

4. Prepare noodles as directed. Drain.

5. Toss noodles and crab mixture together. Pour dressing over and stir to coat.

Yield: 2 servings

FAUX CRAB RAMEN

4	tablespoons butter
1/2	small onion, finely chopped
1	carrot, shredded
1	cup imitation crabmeat
1/2	teaspoon garlic powder
1/4	teaspoon celery seed
1/4	teaspoon Old Bay seasoning
2	packages Top Ramen or Top Ramen Low Fat (no seasoning packet)

1. In a 10-inch skillet, melt butter and sauté onion and carrot until tender.
2. Add crabmeat, garlic powder, celery seed, and Old Bay seasoning. Simmer, stirring occasionally, for about 5 minutes.
3. Prepare noodles as directed. Drain.
4. Remove crab mixture from heat and toss with noodles.

Yield: 2 servings

RAMEN WITH CRABMEAT SAUCE

1	tablespoon olive oil
1	clove garlic, minced
1	small onion, diced
1	small tomato, diced
8	ounces clam juice
1	tablespoon dry sherry
	Dash each pepper and salt
1/2	pound imitation crabmeat
2	packages Top Ramen or Top Ramen Low Fat (no seasoning packet)
1/2	tablespoon chopped parsley

1. In large saucepan, heat olive oil and sauté garlic for about 2 minutes.

2. Add onions and cook until tender.

3. Stir in tomatoes, clam juice, sherry, pepper, and salt.

4. Reduce heat, cover, and simmer about 8 minutes.

5. Stir in crabmeat; heat through.

6. Prepare noodles as directed. Drain. Toss noodles with crab mixture.

7. Sprinkle with chopped parsley.

Yield: 2 servings

SHRIMP BISQUE NOODLES

2	tablespoons butter
1	small onion, chopped
1	small green pepper, chopped
1/4	pound small shrimp, peeled and deveined
2	tablespoons dry sherry
1/2	can (8 ounces) shrimp bisque
1/3	cup heavy cream
2	packages Top Ramen or Top Ramen Low Fat (shrimp flavor)

1. Melt butter in large skillet and sauté onion and pepper until softened.

2. Add shrimp and continue to cook covered about 7 minutes (be careful not to overcook—shrimp should not be tough).

3. Add the dry sherry, shrimp bisque, and cream and continue to cook covered over low heat for 5 more minutes. Remove from heat.

4. Prepare noodles as directed. Drain.

5. Toss shrimp sauce with noodles to fully coat.

Yield: 2 servings

RAMEN WITH
WHITE CLAM SAUCE

2	packages Top Ramen or Top Ramen Low Fat (shrimp or chicken flavor)
2	tablespoons olive oil
2	tablespoons butter
2	cloves garlic, finely chopped
2	cups clam juice (supplement the reserved juice to make up this amount)
1/4	cup white cooking wine
1/4	teaspoon thyme
	Dash black pepper
1	can (10 ounces) chopped clams, drained and juice reserved
1/4	cup dried parsley
	Grated Parmesan cheese

1. Prepare noodles as directed. Drain and set aside.

2. Sauté garlic in butter and oil.

3. Add clam juice, wine, thyme, and pepper. Simmer 8–9 minutes.

4. Stir in clams and parsley; cook for about 1 minute.

5. Pour sauce over hot noodles. Toss to completely coat.

6. Sprinkle Parmesan on top before serving.

Yield: 2 servings

RAMEN WITH RED CLAM SAUCE

2	tablespoons olive oil
2	cloves garlic, finely chopped
1	can (16 ounces) crushed tomatoes in purée
1/2	teaspoon dried oregano
	Dash red pepper flakes
1	can (10 ounces) clams, drained and juice reserved
1/4	cup clam juice (from reserved juice)
1/2	teaspoon sugar
2	packages Top Ramen or Top Ramen Low Fat (no seasoning packet)
	Grated Parmesan cheese

1. Sauté garlic in oil about 20 minutes.

2. Add tomatoes and cook for about 10 minutes or until thickened.

3. Over medium heat, add oregano, pepper, clams, clam juice, and sugar. Continue cooking for 5 minutes and season to taste.

4. Prepare noodles as directed. Drain. Toss noodles with clam sauce.

5. Top with Parmesan cheese and serve.

Yield: 2 servings

SHRIMP THERMIDOR RAMEN

1	stick (8 tablespoons) butter
1/2	pound crabmeat or imitation crab meat
1/2	pound small shrimp, peeled and deveined
1	package (10 ounces) frozen peas
2	packages Top Ramen or Top Ramen Low Fat (shrimp flavor)

1. Melt butter in 2-quart saucepan. Sauté crab and shrimp until shrimp are pink and firm.

2. Meanwhile, boil peas about 7 minutes. Add raw ramen and seasoning packet to peas and boil 3 minutes more. Drain.

3. Add noodle mixture to seafood. Toss to coat.

Yield: 4 servings

CHICKEN CASSEROLE

3	medium raw potatoes, sliced
7	ounces cooked, cubed chicken (canned or fresh)
1	small onion, sliced
2	packages Top Ramen or Top Ramen Low Fat, coarsely broken (chicken flavor)
3	carrots, chopped
1	can condensed cream of chicken soup
1/2	can water or milk
1/4	teaspoon each pepper and paprika

1. Alternate layers of potato, chicken, onions, raw ramen and carrots in a greased casserole dish. Top layer should be potato with ramen on top.

2. Mix together soup, water or milk, spices, and one seasoning packet. Pour mixture over casserole.

3. Bake covered at 375°F for 50 minutes.

4. Bake uncovered for 5–10 more minutes, or until ramen are browned.

≈**NOTE**≈ For variation, subtitute 1 can (6–8 ounces) of fish (tuna or salmon) for the chicken and use a cream of vegetable soup.

Yield: 4 servings

TUNA NOODLE CASSEROLE

2   packages Top Ramen or Top Ramen
        Low Fat, broken into four pieces (any flavor)
2/3   cup chopped celery
1 1/2   tablespoons butter
1   can condensed cheddar cheese soup
1/2   cup milk
1   can (6 1/8 ounces) tuna
2   tablespoons grated Parmesan cheese

1. Prepare all but one piece of ramen (1/4 of 1 package, which you should crush). Drain.

2. In a large saucepan, cook celery in butter until limp.

3. Stir in soup and milk; blend well.

4. Stir in tuna and noodles.

5. Transfer mixture to a nonstick casserole and top with grated cheese and crushed raw ramen.

6. Bake (uncovered) at 375°F for 25 minutes, or until heated through.

Yield: 4 servings

OVERNIGHT RAMEN CHICKEN CASSEROLE

3 cups cooked chicken
2 packages Top Ramen or Top Ramen
  Low Fat, coarsely broken (chicken flavor)
2 cans condensed cream of mushroom soup
1 small onion, chopped
1 teaspoon salt
2 teaspoons lemon juice
1 cup mayonnaise
1 cup chopped celery
4 eggs, hard-boiled and chopped
1/2 cup slivered almonds (optional)
1 small package crushed potato chips

1. Combine all ingredients (except chips) and refrigerate in a nonstick casserole dish overnight.
2. Remove from refrigerator 1 hour before baking.
3. Put crushed chips on top. Bake at 370°F for 40 minutes.

Yield: 4 servings

CHICKEN CARROT NOODLE COMBO

2	tablespoons butter
3/4	cup carrots, finely chopped
1/4	cup green onions, chopped
1	pound skinless, boneless chicken breast, cut into thin strips
1	can condensed cream of vegetable soup
1	cup milk
	Dash pepper
2	packages Top Ramen or Top Ramen Low Fat, coarsely broken (chicken flavor)

1. In a large skillet, melt butter and cook carrots and green onion until tender.
2. Add chicken; cook until browned.
3. Stir in soup, milk, and pepper. Heat to boiling.
4. Reduce heat to low. Cover and simmer about 10 minutes, stirring occasionally.
5. Prepare noodles as directed. Drain.
6. Stir noodles into chicken mixture. Cover and remove from heat. Let stand 5 minutes before serving.

Yield: 4 servings

RAMEN WITH CHICKEN, SPINACH, AND MUSHROOMS

1	tablespoon oil
1/2	boneless chicken breast, cut into thin pieces (about 1 cup)
1/2	cup fresh, sliced mushrooms
1/2	small onion, diced
1	cup water
1/2	package (4 ounces) light cream cheese
1	cup coarsely chopped spinach
1/2	teaspoon coarsely ground black pepper
1	package Top Ramen or Top Ramen Low Fat (chicken flavor)

1. In a 10-inch skillet, heat oil and lightly brown chicken. Remove chicken to a warm plate.

2. In skillet, cook mushrooms and onion until onion is translucent.

3. Add water, seasoning packet, and cream cheese. Heat to boiling, stirring until cream cheese is melted.

4. Stir in chicken, spinach, and black pepper; heat through.

5. Prepare noodles as directed. Drain.

6. Toss noodles with chicken mixture.

Yield: 2 servings

HONEY LEMON CHICKEN AND RAMEN

2	tablespoons oil
1/2	boneless chicken breast, cut up (about 1 cup)
1/4	cup chopped onion
1	cup water
2	tablespoons honey
2	tablespoons lemon juice
	Dash each salt and pepper
1	package Top Ramen or Top Ramen Low Fat (no seasoning packet)

1. In medium saucepan, heat oil and brown chicken chunks until almost done; remove chicken to warm platter.

2. Add onion to pan and cook until translucent.

3. Stir in water, honey, lemon juice, salt, and pepper until evenly blended. Bring mixture to a boil.

4. Add chicken and reduce heat to a simmer.

5. Prepare noodles as directed. Drain.

6. Remove chicken mixture from heat and toss with noodles.

Yield: 1 serving

RAMEN WITH SCALLOPS AND DRIED TOMATOES

1/3 cup sundried tomatoes
1 tablespoon olive oil
1/4 pound medium scallops, rinsed and cleaned
1 tablespoon dried basil
1/2 cup half-and-half
1 package Top Ramen or Top Ramen
Low Fat (no seasoning packet)
Coarsely ground black pepper

1. Place tomatoes in small bowl and pour boiling water over them to cover. Let stand 5 minutes to soften. Remove from water and cut tomatoes into thin strips; set aside.

2. In a 10-inch skillet, heat olive oil and sauté scallops until lightly browned and opaque throughout. Reduce heat.

3. Add basil, cream, and tomatoes to skillet. Heat through and then remove from heat.

4. Prepare noodles as directed. Drain.

5. Toss noodles with scallop mixture. Top with coarsely ground black pepper.

Yield: 1 serving

RAMEN SHRIMP "RISOTTO"

2	packages Top Ramen or Top Ramen Low Fat, finely crushed (shrimp flavor)
2	tablespoons butter
1/2	cup sliced mushrooms
1/3	cup chopped green bell pepper
1 1/2	cups water
1/4	cup dry sherry
1/4	teaspoon dried crushed sage
1/4	pound shrimp, peeled and deveined
2	tablespoons grated Parmesan cheese

1. Prepare noodles as directed, reserving seasoning packet. Drain.

2. In a medium saucepan, melt butter and cook mushrooms and green pepper until tender.

3. Add noodles and sauté 1 minute.

4. Add water, seasoning packets, sherry, and sage. Stir and bring to a boil.

5. Reduce heat to a simmer. Add shrimp and cook until shrimp turn pink and become firm.

6. Remove from heat and sprinkle with Parmesan.

Yield: 2 servings

RAMEN WITH SALMON FILLET AND HERB DRESSING

2   tablespoons butter
1   salmon fillet (about 4 ounces), skin removed
Dressing:
1   tablespoon butter
1   teaspoon garlic powder
1   tablespoon flour
1/4   teaspoon dried crushed oregano
1/8   teaspoon salt
     Dash pepper
3/4   cup milk
1   package Top Ramen or Top Ramen
     Low Fat (no seasoning packet)

1. In 10-inch skillet over medium to high heat, melt butter and cook salmon until golden outside and opaque inside (3 minutes per side). Remove to a warm platter.

2. To make the dressing, melt the butter in a small saucepan. Stir in garlic powder, flour, oregano, salt, and pepper.

3. Add milk all at once. Cook and stir over medium heat till thick and bubbly. Remove from heat and stir one minute more.

4. Prepare noodles as directed. Drain.

5. Place noodles on warm plate. Lay salmon over noodles and pour herb dressing over both.

Yield: 1 serving

RAMEN WITH SHRIMP AND ASPARAGUS

1/2   pound shrimp, peeled and deveined
        Dash crushed red pepper
2   tablespoons lemon juice
        Dash salt
2   tablespoons olive oil, divided
1/2   medium onion, diced
1   yellow bell pepper, julienned
1/2   pound asparagus, cut into 1-inch pieces
1/4   cup water
2   packages Top Ramen or Top Ramen Low Fat (shrimp flavor)

1. In a small bowl, mix shrimp with pepper, lemon juice, and salt.

2. In a 10-inch skillet, heat 1 tablespoon of the oil and sauté onion and yellow pepper for about 3 minutes.

3. Add asparagus to onion mixture and sauté another 3 minutes or until asparagus is tender. Remove vegetables to a warm platter.

4. Add remaining tablespoon oil to skillet. Add shrimp mixture and sauté until shrimp turn pink.

5. Return vegetable mixture to skillet; add water. Heat through.
6. Prepare noodles as directed. Drain.
7. Toss noodles with shrimp and vegetable mixtures.

Yield: 4 servings

RAMEN
CREOLE

3   tablespoons butter
1/2   cup onion, finely chopped
1/4   cup green pepper, finely chopped
1/4   cup celery, finely chopped
1/2   teaspoon cayenne pepper
      Dash black pepper
1   can (8 ounces) tomato sauce
1   cup water
2   cloves garlic, finely chopped
1/2   tablespoon salt
1/4   cup ketchup
1/2   pound small shrimp, peeled and deveined
2   packages Top Ramen or Top Ramen
      Low Fat (shrimp flavor)

1. In a large saucepan or Dutch oven, melt butter and sauté onions, green pepper, and celery.

2. Add cayenne and black pepper and pour in tomato sauce. Simmer about 5 minutes.

3. Next add water, seasoning packet, and garlic. Simmer 5 more minutes.

4. Add salt and ketchup. Simmer 5 more minutes.

5. Add shrimp and cook, stirring occasionally until shrimp are pink and firm.

6. Prepare noodles as directed. Drain. Toss noodles with shrimp mixture.

Yield: 4 servings

PAELLA THE EASY WAY

2	tablespoons oil
2	cloves garlic, finely chopped
1	can (16 ounces) tomatoes, crushed in liquid
1/2	chicken breast, cut up into bite-size pieces (about 1 cup)
1/4	pound uncooked small shrimp, peeled and deveined
1	small can (6–8 ounces) clams, drained
1/4	teaspoon oregano
	Dash cayenne pepper
	Pinch saffron (optional)
2	packages Top Ramen or Top Ramen Low Fat (no seasoning packet)
	Coarsely ground black pepper (garnish)

1. In large skillet, sauté garlic in oil for 2 minutes.

2. Add tomatoes; stir.

3. Add chicken. Cover and simmer over moderate heat for about 10 minutes or until chicken is mostly cooked.

4. Add shrimp and simmer until shrimp turn pink. Add clams, oregano, cayenne pepper, saffron, and simmer 5 minutes more.

5. Prepare noodles as directed. Drain.

6. Toss chicken mixture with noodles and top with black pepper.

CHICKEN, HAM, AND MUSHROOM NOODLES

2	tablespoons butter, divided
1/2	boneless chicken breast, cut in strips (about 1 cup)
2	tablespoons chopped onion
1/2	cup fresh, sliced mushrooms
1/2	small red pepper, julienned
1/3	cup heavy cream
2	tablespoons grated Swiss cheese
1	egg yolk
1	cup cooked ham, cut in julienne strips
2	packages Top Ramen or Top Ramen Low Fat (no seasoning packet)

1. In a 10-inch skillet, heat 1 tablespoon of the butter and sauté chicken strips until lightly browned; remove chicken to warm platter.

2. In skillet, sauté onion, mushrooms, and red pepper for 4 minutes.

3. Add cream to skillet and bring to a boil.

4. Add cheese to skillet and reduce heat to medium. Cook slowly until cheese is completely melted.

5. Turn heat to low, and add egg yolk, the remaining butter, chicken, and ham stirring until heated through.

6. Prepare noodles as directed. Drain.

7. Remove sauce from heat and add ramen; toss to coat.

CAJUN
NOODLES

1/3	cup butter
1	small onion, chopped
1	small red bell pepper, chopped
2	cloves garlic, finely chopped
1	tablespoon jalapeno peppers, finely chopped
	Cayenne pepper and salt to taste
2	tablespoons flour
1/4	cup fresh chopped parsley
1/2	cup half-and-half cream
2	teaspoons lemon juice
8	ounces Velveeta, cubed
1	pound small shrimp, peeled and deveined
1/4	pound crab meat or imitation crab meat
2	packages Top Ramen or Top Ramen Low Fat (no seasoning packet)

1. In a Dutch oven or large saucepan, melt butter. Sauté onions, bell pepper, garlic, and jalapenos for approximately 5 minutes. Add cayenne pepper and salt to taste.

2. Add flour slowly, stirring steadily. Add parsley and cook for 7 more minutes.

3. Add cream, lemon juice, and cheese. Continue to stir until cheese is melted and well blended, but do not boil.

4. In a separate small skillet, panbroil shrimp for 2–3 minutes.
5. Add shrimp and crab meat to cheese mixture and cook about 10 minutes.
6. Prepare noodles as directed. Drain.
7. Stir noodles into cheese-seafood mixture and heat through.

Yield: 4 servings

SALADS AND SIDES

What's a meal without a salad or sidedish? Many of the following salad and sides recipes are easy to prepare quickly for unexpected guests or to add to a meal. Some of them are tangy with vinegar or spices, but you can change the amounts of ingredients to suit your taste.

VEGETABLE RAMEN

1   cup any variety frozen vegetable
1   package Top Ramen or Top Ramen
      Low Fat, coarsely broken (any flavor)
1   tablespoon butter
1/4   teaspoon salt
1/4   teaspoon coarsely ground pepper

1. Boil vegetables according to package directions (5–7 minutes).

2. Add ramen and seasoning packet and continue boiling 3–4 minutes more. Drain.

3. Mix vegetables and noodles with butter until melted. Add salt and pepper.

Yield: 2 servings

RAMEN CELERY MIX

1   package Top Ramen or Top Ramen Low Fat, broken into 4 pieces (chicken flavor)
1/2   cup thinly sliced celery
2   tablespoons water
1   packet hot mustard sauce (1 tablespoon)

1. Prepare noodles as directed, reserving seasoning packet. Drain.
2. In a saucepan over medium heat, cook celery, water, mustard, and seasoning packet (covered) for about 5 minutes, stirring occasionally.
3. Toss celery mixture with noodles.

Yield: 1 serving

RAMEN WITH BROCCOLI AND CHEESE

1   package (10 ounces) frozen broccoli (or
    2 cups fresh)
1   package Top Ramen or Top Ramen
    Low Fat, coarsely broken (any flavor)
1/2 cup condensed cheddar cheese soup
1/4 teaspoon salt
1/4 teaspoon pepper

1. Boil broccoli according to package directions (7–9 minutes or until tender).

2. Add ramen and seasoning packet; boil 3 minutes more. Drain.

3. Mix broccoli and noodles with the soup. Add salt and pepper.

Yield: 2 servings

CLAMMY CARROTS AND RAMEN

1	package Top Ramen or Top Ramen Low Fat (no seasoning packet)
3/4	cup clam juice, divided
2	medium carrots, sliced
1/2	medium onion, sliced
	Salt and coarsely ground black pepper

1. Prepare noodles as directed. Drain.
2. Heat 1/4 cup of the clam juice in 10-inch fry pan. Add carrots and onion and sauté over medium heat for 10 minutes.
3. Add remaining clam juice to the carrot mixture and cook 2 minutes to heat through. Add salt and pepper to taste.
4. Add sauce to noodles and toss.

Yield: 2 servings

RAMEN VINAIGRETTE

1	package Top Ramen or Top Ramen Low Fat noodles (any flavor)
1/4	cup commercial Italian salad dressing
1/2	cup frozen mixed vegetables

1. Prepare noodles as directed. Drain.
2. While noodles are still warm, toss with dressing.
3. Add frozen vegies to the still-warm noodles and leave at room temperature until the vegies are thawed.

Yield: 1 serving

GARLIC RAMEN VINAIGRETTE

1/2	cup vegetable oil
1/3	cup vinegar
1	tablespoon sugar
2	large cloves garlic, minced
1/8	teaspoon pepper
2	packages Top Ramen or Top Ramen Low Fat (no seasoning packet)

1. For dressing, in container with lid, mix all ingredients except ramen and shake vigorously. Refrigerate up to 2 weeks. Shake well before serving.

2. For salad, prepare noodles as directed. Drain.

3. Toss noodles with 1/2 cup of the vinagrette dressing. Serve on bed of lettuce leaves. Top with freshly ground black pepper.

Yield: 2 servings

VEGETABLE NOODLE SALAD

1   package (16 ounces) frozen mixed vegetables (about 2 cups)

1   package Top Ramen or Top Ramen Low Fat, coarsely broken (vegetable flavor)

1   cup canned, drained chick peas

1/2   cup cooked, cubed ham

1/2   cup commercial Italian salad dressing

1. Thaw vegetables.
2. Prepare noodles as directed. Drain.
3. Combine vegetables, noodles, chick peas, and ham in large bowl.
4. Add dressing and toss. Refrigerate at least two hours.

Yield: 4 servings

ITALIAN NOODLE SALAD

2	packages Top Ramen or Top Ramen Low Fat, coarsely broken (no seasoning packet)
1	medium tomato, chopped
1/2	small onion, chopped
1	clove garlic, minced
1	cup commercial Italian salad dressing
1/4	cup grated Parmesan cheese

1. Prepare noodles as directed. Drain. Return to warm pan.
2. In same pan, mix together noodles, tomato, onion, garlic, and dressing.
3. Sprinkle Parmesan over mixture.
4. Serve immediately as warm salad or refrigerate at least two hours for cold salad.

Yield: 2 servings

COLD CUCUMBERS AND NOODLES

1	package Top Ramen or Top Ramen Low Fat, coarsely broken (no seasoning packet)
1/4	cup sour cream
1	teaspoon vinegar
1/4	cup mayonnaise
1	cucumber, julienned
1/4	teaspoon ground pepper

1. Prepare noodles as directed. Drain.
2. Mix noodles with rest of ingredients.
3. Chill for at least 30 minutes.

Yield: 2 servings

RAMENRONI SALAD

2	packages Top Ramen or Top Ramen Low Fat, coarsely broken (no seasoning packet)
1	carrot, finely chopped
1	small onion, finely chopped
2	tablespoons pickle relish
3	eggs, hard-boiled and chopped

Dressing:

1	cup mayonnaise
1 1/2	teaspoons vinegar
2	teaspoons Dijon mustard (or regular mustard)
1/2	teaspoon salt
1/4	teaspoon pepper

1. Prepare noodles as directed. Drain.
2. Combine noodles, carrot, onion, relish, and eggs in a medium bowl.
3. Mix dressing ingredients together and pour over noodle mixture. Stir until coated.
4. Refrigerate at least two hours before serving.

Yield: 4 servings

VG

ORIENTAL
SALAD

1	package Top Ramen or Top Ramen Low Fat noodles, coarsely broken (no seasoning packet)
1/3	cup vegetable oil
1 1/2	tablespoons white vinegar
1/3	cup sugar
1	tablespoon soy sauce
1 1/2	tablespoons sesame seeds

1. Prepare noodles as directed. Drain.

2. In small bowl, mix oil, vinegar, sugar, and soy sauce together until sugar dissolves.

3. Pour oil mixture over noodles to taste (you may want to reserve extra dressing for another day).

4. Sprinkle sesame seeds on top. Chill.

Yield: 2 servings

CRUNCHY ORIENTAL RAMEN SALAD

2	packages Top Ramen or Top Ramen Low Fat, crushed (oriental flavor)
1	medium carrot, finely chopped or slivered
1/2	cup scallions, chopped
1	can (8 ounce) water chestnuts, drained
1	can (8 ounce) bamboo shoots, drained
1/2	cup canned chopped mushrooms, drained
1/2	cup soy sauce
1	tablespoon sesame seeds (optional)

1. Mix together all ingredients.
2. Refrigerate for at least 2 hours.

Yield: 4 servings

CHEF SALAD
WITH RAMEN

2   packages Top Ramen or Top Ramen Low Fat, coarsely broken (no seasoning packet)
4–6   large leaves of iceberg lettuce
2   cups Swiss cheese, julienned
1 3/4 cups ham lunchmeat, julienned
1 3/4 cups turkey lunchmeat, julienned
2   eggs, hard-boiled and sliced
      Any flavor commercial creamy salad dressing

1. Prepare noodles as directed. Drain.
2. Line a large glass bowl with the lettuce leaves.
3. Top with half of the noodles.
4. Top noodles with half of the cheese, ham, and turkey. Repeat layers.
5. Top with egg slices.
6. Drizzle dressing over salad and refrigerate for at least 1 hour before serving.

Yield: 4 servings

CHINESE CHICKEN SALAD

1	head iceberg lettuce, shredded
2	cups cooked chicken, shredded
3	carrots, shredded
1	red pepper, chopped
4	green onions, chopped
1	package Top Ramen or Top Ramen Low Fat, crushed (no seasoning packet)

Dressing:

3	tablespoons rice vinegar (or white vinegar)
1	packet soy sauce (1 tablespoon)
2	tablespoons sesame oil
2	tablespoons vegetable oil
	Salt and pepper to taste

1. In a large glass bowl, combine lettuce, chicken, carrots, red pepper, and onions.
2. In a small bowl, mix all dressing ingredients.
3. Pour dressing over salad; toss.
4. Crumble in raw noodles just before serving and mix well.

Yield: 4–6 servings

LAYERED RAMEN VEGETABLE SALAD

1	package Top Ramen or Top Ramen Low Fat, crushed (no seasoning packet)
2	cups lettuce, shredded or torn up
1	medium tomato, chopped
1	medium cucumber, sliced
2	medium carrots, sliced
1	package (6 ounces) pepperoni slices
1	cup cubed mozzarella cheese
2	cups commercial Italian salad dressing

1. Prepare noodles as directed. Drain.

2. In a large glass bowl, arrange layers in this order: lettuce (on the bottom), cooked noodles, tomato, cucumber, carrots, pepperoni, and cheese.

3. Pour dressing over salad and refrigerate at least 2 hours so that dressing filters throughout layers.

Yield: 4 servings

LAYERED RAMEN ANTIPASTO SALAD

1   package Top Ramen or Top Ramen
         Low Fat (1/2 vegetable or chicken flavor)
1   cup cauliflower florets
1   carrot, sliced
1/2   cup canned green beans
1/4   cup pickled onions, cut in half
1/4   cup green olives stuffed with pimentos
1   dill pickle, chopped
1/2   medium green pepper, chopped
3   anchovies

Dressing:
1   cup ketchup
1/2   cup chili sauce
3   tablespoons vegetable oil
3   tablespoons vinegar
         Pinch of salt

1. Prepare noodles as directed, using only 1/2 packet seasoning. Drain.

2. Combine dressing ingredients in a small bowl; set aside.

3. In a large glass bowl, place the noodles on the bottom as the first layer.

4. Layer the other ingredients, alternating colors and textures.

5. Top with the dressing. Refrigerate at least 2 hours before serving.

Yield: 4 servings

1, 2, 3 RAMEN AND CABBAGE SALAD

1	very small head of cabbage, finely chopped (about 2 cups)
5	scallions, chopped
2	medium carrots, grated or julienned
1	package Top Ramen or Top Ramen Low Fat, crushed (no seasoning packet)
1/2	cup sliced almonds
1/4	cup sunflower seeds
1/2	cup plus 1 tablespoon vegetable oil, divided
4	tablespoons rice vinegar (or other vinegar)
2	tablespoons sugar
1/2	teaspoon salt
1/2	teaspoon pepper

1. In medium bowl, mix together cabbage, scallion, carrots, and crumbled raw noodles. Set aside.

2. Stir-fry almonds and sunflower seeds in 1 tablespoon of the oil. Mix with the vegetable mixture.

3. Mix the remaining 1/2 cup of oil with vinegar, sugar, and spices and pour over cabbage mixture.

4. Refrigerate in a covered container overnight (or at least 10 hours), so noodles soak up dressing and soften.

Yield: 4 servings

CHINESE COLESLAW

Dressing:

2/3   cup vegetable oil
6   tablespoons vinegar
1/4   cup sugar
       Salt and pepper to taste
4   tablespoons sesame seeds

Slaw:

2   packages Top Ramen or Top Ramen Low Fat, coarsely broken (no seasoning packet)
1   small head of cabbage, shredded (about 3 cups)
3   green onions, chopped
1/3   cup slivered almonds

1. In small bowl, mix together oil, vinegar, sugar, salt, pepper, and sesame seeds.

2. Crumble raw noodles into dressing; let sit 5 minutes.

3. In another bowl, combine cabbage, onions, and almonds. Pour dressing mixture over cabbage mixture. Chill for at least 2 hours; best if left overnight.

Yield: 4 servings

CHINESE BROCCOLI NOODLE SALAD

2	packages Top Ramen or Top Ramen Low Fat, coarsely broken (no seasoning packet)
1	cucumber, sliced
2	cups cooked broccoli, cut up
1	small can mandarin orange slices (11 ounces), drained
1/2	cup unsalted peanuts

Dressing:

1/3	cup rice vinegar (or other vinegar)
1	tablespoon sugar
2	teaspoons sesame oil
1	teaspoon chili powder
1/3	cup vegetable oil
	Salt to taste

1. Prepare noodles as directed. Drain and rinse with cold water.

2. Mix dressing ingredients in small bowl until sugar and salt are dissolved.

3. In a large glass bowl, layer the salad as follows: noodles, cucumbers, broccoli, mandarin oranges, and peanuts.

4. Pour the dressing over mixture the the salad.

Yield: 2 servings

NUTTY FRUIT SALAD

2	packages Top Ramen or Top Ramen Low Fat, coarsely broken (no seasoning packet)
1	container (8 ounces) peach yogurt
1	small can mandarin oranges (11 ounces), drained
1	cup seedless red grapes
1	cup seedless green grapes
1	medium apple, peeled, cored, and chopped
1/2	cup walnut halves

1. Prepare noodles as directed. Drain and rinse with cold water.
2. Combine all ingredients and toss to coat everything with yogurt.
3. Chill at least 1 hour.

Yield: 2 servings

COLD HAM AND NOODLE SALAD

2	packages Top Ramen or Top Ramen Low Fat, crushed (pork flavor)
3	tablespoons mayonnaise
1	tablespoon mustard
1	teaspoon salt
1/2	teaspoon pepper
1/2	small onion, chopped
1	cup chopped cooked ham

1. Prepare noodles as directed. Drain.
2. In small bowl, mix mayonnaise, mustard, salt, and pepper .
3. In a large bowl, mix noodles, onion, and ham.
4. Pour mayonnaise mixture over noodle mixture. Toss until coated.

Yield: 2 servings

RAMEN AND CHICKEN BREAST SALAD

2	packages Top Ramen or Top Ramen Low Fat, coarsely broken (chicken flavor)
2	cups cooked chicken breast, cubed
1	package (10 ounces) frozen chopped spinach, thawed and drained
2	cups seedless green grapes, halved
2	tablespoons grated Parmesan cheese
1/2	teaspoon salt
1	tablespoon olive oil
1	tablespoon red wine vinegar
1/2	teaspoon coarsely ground black pepper

1. Prepare noodles as directed. Drain and rinse with cold water.
2. In a large bowl, toss noodles with rest of ingredients until all are coated.

Yield: 4 servings

SEAFOOD NOODLE SALAD

2	packages Top Ramen or Top Ramen Low Fat, coarsely broken (shrimp flavor)
2	cups crabmeat or imitation crabmeat (or precooked shrimp)
3	tablespoons mayonnaise
2	tablespoons mustard
2	teaspoons Old Bay seasoning
1	teaspoon celery seed
	Dash each salt and pepper

1. Prepare noodles as directed. Drain.
2. Mix noodles and seafood.
3. In small bowl, stir together mayonnaise, mustard, Old Bay, celery seed, salt, and pepper.
4. Toss noodle mixture with dressing until evenly coated.

Yield: 4 servings

MEXICAN SALSA SALAD

1	package Top Ramen or Top Ramen Low Fat, crushed (no seasoning packet)
1	small tomato, chopped
1	small onion, chopped
3	cloves garlic, finely chopped
1/4	cup fresh cilantro, chopped
1/4	cup chopped green chili peppers
1/4	cup chopped red chili peppers
1	tablespoon sour cream
	Couple slices of jalapeno peppers

1. Prepare noodles as directed. Drain and chill.

2. Mix tomato, onion, garlic, cilantro, green chilis, and red chilis in small bowl. Refrigerate for at least 2 hours.

3. Stir noodles into chilled tomato mixture.

4. Before serving, put sour cream on top of salad and top with jalapeno slices.

Yield: 2 servings

RAMEN WITH SPICY PEANUT BUTTER

1	package Top Ramen or Top Ramen Low Fat noodles (oriental flavor)
1	tablespoon butter
1	small onion, finely chopped
1	clove garlic, minced
2	tablespoons oil
1/3	cup smooth peanut butter
1	teaspoon flaked red pepper
2	tablespoons lemon juice
2	tablespoons soy sauce
1/2	cup water

1. Prepare noodles as directed reserving seasoning packet. Drain.

2. In a medium fry pan, fry the onion in butter until translucent; then add garlic and sauté for about 1 minute. Keep in pan but remove from heat.

3. With blender, mix rest of ingredients and 1/2 teaspoon of the seasoning packet until smooth.

4. Add peanut butter mixture to garlic and onion in warm pan.

5. Toss cooked noodles with peanut butter mixture until noodles are coated.

≈**NOTE**≈ This recipe can be dressed up by adding any of the following: steamed carrots, broccoli, green beans, cabbage, chopped egg, apple, raisins, toasted nuts, sesame seed oil, sliced chicken breast, shrimp, fish, or leftover steak.

Yield: 1 serving

RAMEN
FRITTERS

1	package Top Ramen or Top Ramen Low Fat noodles, crushed (no seasoning packet)
3	tablespoons vegetable oil, divided
3	green onions, finely chopped
1/4	cup flour
2	tablespoons grated Parmesan cheese
1/2	teaspoon salt
1/4	teaspoon ground black pepper
1	egg
1/4	cup water

1. Prepare noodles as directed. Drain.

2. Sauté green onions in 1 tablespoon of the oil until tender. Remove from heat.

3. In a medium bowl, whisk flour, Parmesan, salt, pepper, egg, and water. Stir in green onions and noodles until well coated.

4. In a 10-inch fry pan with sides, heat the remaining 2 tablespoons of the oil until very hot. Into hot oil, drop mixture by 1/4 cup mounds about 2 inches apart. With pancake turner, flatten each mound slightly.

5. Cook fritters until golden brown on both sides.
6. Remove to paper towels to drain; keep warm. Repeat with remaining fritter mixture.

Yield: about 8 fritters

FANCY CHICKEN AND RAMEN SALAD WITH CITRUS

1	cup cottage cheese
1/3	cup orange juice
1 1/2	teaspoons white wine vinegar
3/4	teaspoon dried basil, crushed
1/2	teaspoon salt
1/4	teaspoon pepper
1/4	teaspoon grated orange zest
2	packages Top Ramen or Top Ramen Low Fat, coarsely broken (no seasoning packet)
2	cups cooked, diced chicken breast
1	small tomato, diced
1	tablespoon dried parsley
	Iceberg lettuce leaves

1. In blender, purée the cottage cheese, juice, vinegar, basil, salt, and pepper until smooth; stir in orange zest.
2. Prepare noodles as directed. Drain.
3. Stir cooked noodles into cottage cheese mixture.
4. Stir in chicken, tomato, and parsley.
5. Refrigerate at least 1 hour.
6. Serve salad on a bed of lettuce leaves.

BREAKFAST AND BRUNCH

Start your day the Top Ramen way! Ramen noodles are an easy and interesting addition to many standard breakfast meals. We've come up with some new and different types of breakfasts, too. Also, you can use the sweet recipes for desserts or use the non-sweet recipes for lunch or dinner.

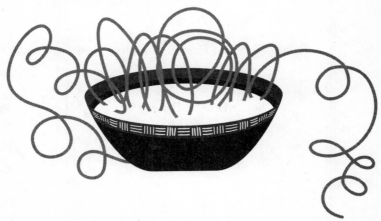

RAMEN WITH
FRIED POTATOES

1 package Top Ramen or Top Ramen
  Low Fat (any flavor)
1 baking potato
1 tablespoon olive oil
1/4 teaspoon garlic salt
  Hot pepper flakes to taste
  Grated Parmesan cheese

1. Prepare noodles as directed. Drain.

2. Microwave potato until you can pierce it easily with a fork (or use a leftover baked potato). Chop potato into half-inch pieces.

3. Heat oil and spices and fry the potato pieces until crisp, stirring occasionally.

4. Add the cooked noodles to the potato mixture. Serve with grated Parmesan cheese.

Yield: 1 serving

RAMEN TOMATO BREAKFAST

1	package Top Ramen or Top Ramen Low Fat, coarsely broken (any flavor)
1	egg
2	tablespoons milk
	Dash pepper
1	tomato, diced

1. Prepare noodles as directed. Drain.

2. Whisk together egg, milk, and pepper.

3. Place egg mixture, tomato, and noodles in a hot fry pan and scramble to desired firmness.

Yield: 2 servings

SWEET RAMEN BREAKFAST

1	cup apple juice
1	cup water
1	package Top Ramen or Top Ramen Low Fat (no seasoning packet)
1/3	cup raisins
1/2	teaspoon each sugar and cinnamon

1. Bring apple juice and water to a boil in a small saucepan. Add noodles to juice mixture; boil for 3 minutes.

2. Add the raisins to the boiling noodle mixture for the last few seconds (to plump them up) and drain.

3. Top hot noodles with sugar and cinnamon.

Yield: 1 serving

STICKY, SWEET RAMEN

2	packages Top Ramen or Top Ramen Low Fat (no seasoning packet)
1	tablespoon butter
1 1/2	tablespoons milk
1/4	cup pancake syrup
3	tablespoons brown sugar

1. Prepare noodles as directed. Drain.
2. In a 1-quart saucepan, melt remaining ingredients over low heat, stirring frequently.
3. Pour mixture over noodles and serve warm.

Yield: 2 servings

RAMEN
BREAKFAST MIX

2	packages Top Ramen or Top Ramen Low Fat (any flavor)
1/2	onion, sliced
1	tablespoon butter
2	cooked sliced potatoes
1/2	teaspoon paprika
	Salt and pepper to taste

1. Prepare noodles as directed. Drain.

2. Sauté onions in butter until translucent.

3. Add cooked potatoes, ramen, and spices to fry pan. Cook for 5 minutes or until heated through.

Yield: 2 servings

RAMEN
OMELET

1   package Top Ramen or Top Ramen
      Low Fat noodles (any flavor)
3   eggs
      Salt and pepper to taste
1   tablespoon butter

1. Prepare noodles as directed, reserving seasoning packet. Drain and mix with seasoning packet. (Store noodles in the fridge for later use. You only need half for this recipe.)

2. Beat the eggs and spices in a bowl. For a really fluffy omelet, separate the eggs, beat the whites until stiff, then fold in the beaten yolks, salt, and pepper.

3. Coat a hot fry pan with the butter and pour in the egg mixture. Reduce the heat to medium-low.

4. When the eggs are almost set, add the ramen noodles.

5. Run a spatula around the outside of the omelet to loosen it, then fold it over on itself (if you fail at this maneuver, just break up the pieces and you have scrambled eggs and ramen).

≈**NOTE**≈ Add variety to this recipe by adding cheese, chopped ham or sausage, or leftover Chinese food.

Yield: 2 serving

CHEESE RAMEN
OMELET

1/2   package Top Ramen or Top Ramen
        Low Fat, crushed (any flavor)
1   tablespoon butter
2   eggs beaten
        Salt and pepper to taste
2   slices American or cheddar cheese

1. Prepare noodles as directed. Drain.
2. Pour eggs into a hot nonstick skillet. Add salt and pepper.
3. When eggs are almost set, place noodles and cheese on one side of omelet.
4. Fold in half and flip once.

Yield: 1 serving

EGGLESS RAMEN "OMELET"

1	package Top Ramen or Top Ramen Low Fat (any flavor)
1/3	cup chopped tomatoes
1/3	cup sliced mushrooms
1/3	cup sliced scallions
2	slices American or cheddar cheese

1. Prepare noodles as directed. Drain.
2. Prepare "Fried Ramen" recipe (see page 31).
3. When noodles are done to desired brownness, place vegetables on half of the noodles.
4. Lay cheese on top of the vegies.
5. Fold over noodles in half like a traditional omelet.
6. Flip once carefully.

Yield: 1 serving

FRIED EGG
RAMEN

1	package Top Ramen or Top Ramen Low Fat (any flavor)
1	tablespoon butter
1	egg
1	slice of cheese

1. Prepare noodles as directed. Drain.
2. Melt butter on medium heat in a fry pan and arrange the ramen in a ring around the outside. Reduce heat to low. When the noodles begin to get crisp on the bottom after (about 15 minutes), break an egg into the middle of the ring.
3. Cover the pan and cook for about 5 minutes (or until the egg is done to your liking).
4. Just prior to serving, add the slice of cheese to the top and replace the lid for a few minutes until the cheese is melted.

Yield: 1 serving

NEST
OF FIRE

1	package Top Ramen or Top Ramen Low Fat, broken into 4 pieces (any flavor)
3	tablespoons salsa
1	egg, poached
	Handful of sliced grapes

1. Prepare noodles as directed. Drain and place in a bowl.
2. Spoon salsa over noodles and place poached egg on top.
3. Garnish with grape slices.

≈**NOTE**≈ To poach the egg, break an egg into a cup. Bring 3 cups of water to a simmer and gently slide egg into the water. Simmer for 3–5 minutes. Remove egg with a slotted spoon.

Yield: 1 serving

BREAKFAST
PASTA

1	package Top Ramen or Top Ramen Low Fat (vegetable or chicken flavor)
2	eggs, scrambled and sliced into thin strips
1/3	cup chopped tomatoes
1/3	cup chopped onion
1/3	cup chopped zucchini
1/3	cup shredded mozzarella
1/4	cup sliced black olives (optional)
	Salt and pepper to taste

1. Prepare noodles as directed. Drain. Return to 2-quart saucepan.
2. Mix together all ingredients over medium heat to melt cheese.

Yield: 2 servings

BREAKFAST
PIZZA

1	package Top Ramen or Top Ramen Low Fat (any flavor)
1/3	cup spaghetti sauce
1	egg, scrambled
1/2	cup shredded mozzarella
1/4	cup sliced mushrooms (optional)

1. Prepare noodles as directed. Drain.
2. Prepare "Fried Ramen" (see page 31).
3. When noodles are almost done (about 12 minutes), spread spaghetti sauce to within 1/2 inch of the sides of the noodles.
4. Top the sauce with the egg, cheese, and mushrooms.
5. Cover the pan and cook for approximately 5 minutes, or until cheese melts.
6. Remove from heat and let stand 5 minutes before serving.

Yield: 1 serving

FARMER'S BREAKFAST RAMEN

1   package Top Ramen or Top Ramen Low Fat, crushed (any flavor)
4   eggs
1 1/2   tablespoons milk
   Dash pepper
1/2   cup cooked, diced ham
1   tablespoon butter
1/2   cup cooked, chopped potato
1/4   cup chopped scallions

1. Prepare noodles as directed. Drain.
2. Whisk together eggs, milk, and pepper. Stir ham and noodles into egg mixture.
3. In skillet, fry potato and scallions in butter, about 5 minutes.
4. Pour egg mixture over potatoes and onions.
5. Cook in skillet without stirring. Occasionally lift the sides so that the unset middle eggs slide to the sides and cook. The meal is finished when the eggs are set, but still glossy.

Yield: 4 servings

RAMEN FRITTATA

1	package Top Ramen or Top Ramen Low Fat, crushed (any flavor)
2	tablespoons olive oil, divided
1	clove garlic, minced
1/2	cup onion, minced
1	small cooked, cubed potato
3	eggs
	Salt and pepper to taste

1. Prepare noodles as directed, reserving the seasoning packet. Drain.

2. Heat 1 tablespoon of the oil in a skillet. Add the garlic, onion, and seasoning packet; sauté until onions are translucent.

3. Stir in potato and noodles, heat 1 minute.

4. Beat the eggs, remaining oil, salt, and pepper together and pour onto potato mixture. Cook until eggs are set.

5. Slide the frittata out of skillet onto large plate. With the plate in your right hand, place the skillet (in your left hand) inverted, on top of the plate and turn both hands so that the eggs flip back into the pan. The uncooked side should now be on the bottom of the pan.

6. Cook 2 more minutes, or until bottom is browned.

≈**NOTE**≈ For variety, add 2 slices cooked crumbled bacon and 1/3 cup fresh chopped spinach to mixture before eggs are set.

Yield: 2 servings

POTATO, EGG, AND RAMEN CASSEROLE

1/2   cup sour cream
1/4   cup butter, softened
1/4   teaspoon each salt and pepper
4   cooked, sliced potatoes
3   eggs, hard-boiled and sliced
1   package Top Ramen or Top Ramen
       Low Fat, crushed (no seasoning packet)

1. Grease a casserole dish.
2. Mix together sour cream, butter, salt and pepper (reserve 1/2 of the mixture).
3. Layer the potatoes, then eggs, then sour cream mixture in the casserole.
4. Cover the top layer of the casserole with the reserved sour cream mixture. Top with raw crushed ramen.
5. Bake at 350°F for 25 minutes, or until heated through.

Yield: 4 servings

RAMEN KUGEL

2	packages Top Ramen or Top Ramen Low Fat, crushed (no seasoning packet)
2	eggs
2	tablespoons sugar
3	tablespoons butter, softened, divided
2	teaspoons baking powder
2	teaspoons vanilla
1	cup raisins
1	small apple, peeled and diced
1/2	teaspoon cinnamon

1. Prepare noodles as directed. Drain.
2. Beat eggs until foamy; slowly add sugar and 1 1/2 tablespoons of the butter; mix well.
3. Add baking powder and vanilla to egg mixture and blend well.
4. Add noodles, raisins, and apple and coat with egg mixture.
5. Coat a small casserole with the remaining butter.
6. Pour mixture into casserole and top with cinnamon.
7. Bake at 375°F for 20–30 minutes, or until top looks brown and crispy. Cool and serve.

Yield: 2 servings

SUPER BRUNCH BAKE

2	medium tomatoes
2	tablespoons butter
1	small onion, chopped
1	clove garlic, minced
1/2	pound ground beef
1 1/2	tablespoons flour
1/2	teaspoon each chili powder and pepper
1	package Top Ramen or Top Ramen Low Fat, crushed (beef flavor)
4	eggs
1/4	cup shredded cheese

1. Halve tomatoes and scoop out centers (reserve).

2. In a skillet melt butter, add onion and garlic. Sauté until onions are limp.

3. Add ground beef and tomato pulp and cook for 10 minutes, stirring frequently.

4. Combine flour, spices, and raw ramen. Stir into meat and tomato mixture and cook 3 minutes more.

5. Pour meat and noodle mixture into baking dish. Arrange tomato halves (round sides down) in mixture.

6. Crack one egg into each tomato half and top with cheese.

7. Bake uncovered at 350°F for 20 minutes, or until eggs are set.

Yield: 4 servings

DESSERTS

Here are some sweet and not-so-sweet desserts using Top Ramen noodles. We think these are great desserts—but we also suggest trying some of them for easy and refreshing lunches. Feel free to add more sugar or experiment with different varieties of fruits.

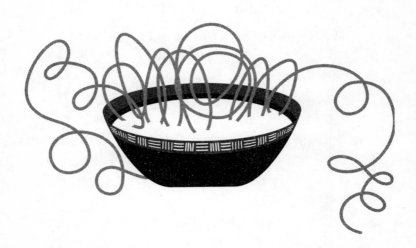

RAMEN WITH CHOCOLATE SAUCE

1	package Top Ramen or Top Ramen Low Fat (no seasoning packet)
2	tablespoons chocolate syrup

Homemade chocolate sauce:

4	ounces milk chocolate pieces
1	tablespoon butter
1/2	cup milk

1. Prepare noodles as directed. Drain.
2. Add syrup to noodles and serve warm.

≈**NOTE**≈ If you would like to make your own chocolate sauce, in a small saucepan melt together the milk chocolate pieces, butter, and milk.

Yield: 1 serving

FRESH FRUIT AND NOODLE TOSS

1   package Top Ramen or Top Ramen
    Low Fat, crushed (no seasoning packet)
1   cup of any of the following:
    blueberries
    raspberries
    strawberries, sliced
    bananas, sliced
    kiwi, sliced
    mandarin orange slices
    fresh cherries, pitted and stems removed

Optional garnishes:
1   tablespoon flaked coconut
1   tablespoon slivered almonds
2   teaspoons powdered sugar

1. Prepare noodles as directed. Drain.
2. Toss with fruit.
3. Top with garnish.

Yield: 1 serving

FRUIT AND NOODLE TOSS WITH YOGURT SAUCE

1   package Top Ramen or Top Ramen
       Low Fat (no seasoning packet)
1   cup fresh fruit
1   container (8 ounces) yogurt (same or comple
       mentary flavor to fruit)

1. Prepare noodles as directed. Drain.
2. Mix noodles with fruit and yogurt.
3. Chill for at least 1 hour before serving.

Yield: 1 serving

COCONUT-CHOCOLATE RAMEN

1   package Top Ramen or Top Ramen
         Low Fat (no seasoning packet)
1   teaspoon salt
1/4   cup coconut (sweetened or unsweetened,
         fresh or toasted)
1   plain chocolate bar (about 1.45 ounces),
         broken or 3 tablespoons chocolate syrup

1. Prepare noodles as directed. Drain. Add salt.
2. In a small frying pan, prepare "Fried Ramen" (see page 31).
3. When noodles are done to desired brownness on bottom, cover the top with coconut. On top of coconut, place pieces of chocolate bar.
4. When chocolate bar melts, remove from heat and serve. If using chocolate syrup, serve immediately.

Yield: 1 serving

APRICOT RAMEN

1   package Top Ramen or Top Ramen
Low Fat, crushed (no seasoning packet)
1   apricot, sliced
1/2   cup cream or whole milk
1   teaspoon brown sugar
Pinch of cinnamon

1. Prepare noodles as directed. Drain.
2. Mix noodles and apricot slices.
3. Pour cream or milk over mixture; add sugar and cinnamon. Stir until coated and serve.

Yield: 1 serving

STRAWBERRY RAMEN

1   package Top Ramen or Top Ramen
     Low Fat, crushed (no seasoning packet)
1   cup sliced strawberries, tops removed
1/2 cup cream or whole milk
1   teaspoon sugar

1. Prepare noodles as directed. Drain.
2. Mix all ingredients together.
3. Stir until well coated before serving.

Yield: 1 serving

PEACHY
RAMEN

1   package Top Ramen or Top Ramen
          Low Fat, crushed (no seasoning packet)
1   medium peach, pitted and sliced
1   cup light cream or whole milk
1/4   cup sugar (brown or white)

1. Preheat oven to 350°F.
2. In small nonstick casserole dish, mix all ingredients making sure raw noodles are covered with cream. Bake for 10 minutes.

Yield: 1 serving

BAKED APPLE
RAMEN

1	medium apple, peeled and sliced
1	package Top Ramen or Top Ramen Low Fat, crushed (no seasoning packet)
1/3	cup raisins
1/2	cup cream or whole milk
1	teaspoon brown sugar
1/2	teaspoon cinnamon

1. Preheat oven to 350°F.

2. Place apple slices on bottom of a small greased casserole dish; top with crushed raw noodles. Sprinkle raisins over noodles.

3. Pour cream over layers. Sprinkle brown sugar and cinnamon on top.

4. Bake for 20 minutes or until warmed through and noodles are soft.

Yield: 2 servings

WARM RAMEN PUDDING WITH RAISINS

3	cups milk
1	package Top Ramen or Top Ramen Low Fat, crushed (no seasoning packet)
1/3	cup raisins
1/4	cup sugar
1	teaspoon vanilla
1/4	teaspoon ground nutmeg

1. In medium saucepan, bring milk to a boil.
2. Stir in ramen and raisins. Cover and cook over low heat for about 15 minutes or until milk is reduced.
3. Stir in sugar and vanilla.
4. Spoon into dessert dishes. Sprinkle with nutmeg. Serve warm.

Yield: 2 servings

RAMEN
CUSTARD

1	package Top Ramen or Top Ramen Low Fat, crushed (no seasoning packet)
3	eggs
1/2	tablespoon instant coffee
1 1/2	cups cottage cheese
1/2	cup plain yogurt
1	teaspoon cinnamon
2	tablespoons sugar
1	tablespoon butter, cut in little bits

1. Prepare noodles as directed. Drain.
2. Combine noodles and rest of ingredients except butter and spread in small buttered casserole.
3. Dot with butter.
4. Bake at 375°F degrees for 35 minutes. Let stand 10 minutes before serving.

≈**NOTE**≈ For variety, try adding salted nuts, 1/2 cup raisins, or sliced apples to this recipe. You may substitute instant custard for the eggs, cheese, and yogurt. Bake as above.

Yield: 4–6 servings

CHOCOLATE RAMEN CUSTARD

1	package Top Ramen or Top Ramen Low Fat, crushed (no seasoning packet)
2	cups scalded milk
$1/2$	cup cocoa
$3/4$	cup sugar
$1/2$	teaspoon instant coffee
2	eggs
2	tablespoons melted butter
$1/2$	cup crushed Oreos (optional)

1. Cover uncooked noodles with scalded milk and let stand for 15 minutes.

2. Mix cocoa, sugar, and instant coffee together; then add to cooled milk and noodles.

3. Add eggs and butter to the noodle mix. Add Oreos.

4. Pour mixture into a shallow buttered casserole dish. Place casserole in larger pan with about $1/2$ inch water in it. Bake at 350°F degrees for 35 minutes or until thin skin forms on top. Let cool at least 10 minutes before serving.

≈**NOTE**≈ For scalded milk, rinse small saucepan in cold water (to keep milk from sticking). Pour milk into cool saucepan and heat over a low flame until it just begins to simmer but doesn't boil. A skin may form on top.

Yield: 4–6 servings

NOODLES
WITH NUTS

2	packages Top Ramen or Top Ramen Low Fat (no seasoning packet)
2/3	cup finely chopped walnuts
1/4	cup confectioner's sugar
1 1/2	tablespoons melted butter
1	teaspoon lemon juice
1/2	teaspoon grated lemon peel

1. Prepare noodles as directed. Drain.

2. Mix walnuts and confectioner's sugar together; set aside.

3. Toss cooked noodles with butter, lemon juice, and lemon peel.

4. Top each serving of the noodle mixture with some of the walnut mixture.

Yield: 2 servings

NOODLES WITH COTTAGE CHEESE AND BACON

1	package Top Ramen or Top Ramen Low Fat, broken into 4 pieces (no seasoning packet)
2	slices bacon
1/3	cup firmly packed cottage cheese, drained
1	tablespoon sour cream
1/4	teaspoon paprika
1/4	teaspoon salt

1. Prepare nooodles as directed. Drain.
2. Pan fry the bacon, reserving the fat. Crumble bacon and set aside.
3. Mix together cottage cheese, sour cream, paprika, and salt. Set aside.
4. In a medium bowl, toss noodles with reserved bacon fat.
5. Top noodles with cottage cheese mixture and sprinkle with crumbled bacon.

≈**NOTE**≈ This is a traditional Hungarian dessert. We know it sounds weird, but try it! We love it.

Yield: 2 servings

ONE FREE BAG

DEALER: Invoices proving purchase of sufficient stock to cover coupons presented must be shown on request. Failure to do so voids all coupons. Coupons may not be transferred or reproduced. Sales tax must be paid by customer. Void where prohibited, taxed or restricted. Nissin Foods will redeem this coupon for its face value plus 8¢ handling if used to redeem one package of any flavor Top Ramen. For payment, mail this coupon to Nissin Foods, P.O. Box 880631, El Paso, TX 88588-0631. Cash redemption value 1/100th-cent. Limit one per purchase.

NO EXPIRATION DATE

LIMIT ONE COUPON PER PURCHASE. MAXIMUM VALUE – $0.25

nissin **Top Ramen.**

5 70662 40001 7

ONE FREE CUP

DEALER: Invoices proving purchase of sufficient stock to cover coupons presented must be shown on request. Failure to do so voids all coupons. Coupons may not be transferred or reproduced. Sales tax must be paid by customer. Void where prohibited, taxed or restricted. Nissin Foods will redeem this coupon for its face value plus 8¢ handling if used to redeem one Cup Noodles any flavor. For payment, mail this coupon to Nissin Foods, P.O. Box 880631, El Paso, TX 88588-0631. Cash redemption value 1/100th-cent. Limit one per purchase.

NO EXPIRATION DATE

LIMIT ONE COUPON PER PURCHASE. MAXIMUM VALUE – $0.60

nissin **CUP NOODLES.**

5 70662 10001 6

ONE FREE BAG

DEALER: Invoices proving purchase of sufficient stock to cover coupons presented must be shown on request. Failure to do so voids all coupons. Coupons may not be transferred or reproduced. Sales tax must be paid by customer. Void where prohibited, taxed or restricted. Nissin Foods will redeem this coupon for its face value plus 8¢ handling if used to redeem one package of any flavor Mug Noodles. For payment, mail this coupon to Nissin Foods, P.O. Box 880631, El Paso, TX 88588-0631. Cash redemption value 1/100th-cent. Limit one per purchase.

NO EXPIRATION DATE

LIMIT ONE COUPON PER PURCHASE. MAXIMUM VALUE – $1.60

nissin **MUG NOODLES**™

5 70662 60001 1

ONE FREE BAG

DEALER: Invoices proving purchase of sufficient stock to cover coupons presented must be shown on request. Failure to do so voids all coupons. Coupons may not be transferred or reproduced. Sales tax must be paid by customer. Void where prohibited, taxed or restricted. Nissin Foods will redeem this coupon for its face value plus 8¢ handling if used to redeem one package of any flavor Top Ramen Low Fat. For payment, mail this coupon to Nissin Foods, P.O. Box 880631, El Paso, TX 88588-0631. Cash redemption value 1/100th-cent. Limit one per purchase.

NO EXPIRATION DATE

LIMIT ONE COUPON PER PURCHASE. MAXIMUM VALUE – $0.25

nissin **Top Ramen.**
LOWFAT

5 70662 70001 8